Otherness in a Fragmented World

This book explores a key theme both for humanity and for psychotherapy—how we can understand ourselves as a web of relational connections within the wider world that shapes us all.

Grounds are the often-invisible scenery of our life. They are all that concern us as human beings—the sum total of relationships, events, all that happens and has happened, our conquests, and our connections, together with what is unfinished and what has yet to emerge. Moving within a horizon of phenomenology and Gestalt therapy, the author explores how we are continuously built and kept alive through our unceasing engagement with otherness—whether cultural, social, linguistic, gender or otherwise, and thus how humanity is intrinsically made by otherness, novelty, and challenging experiences that transform us in a way we can never anticipate. At the same time, we also define ourselves by identifying with certain groups which become part of who we see ourselves as being. Here the aim is to describe and connect the forms of suffering and the creative adjustments found today with the grounds from which they emerge, rather than with the figures that stand out more visibly and can blind us.

Drawing on extensive clinical practice and a deep understanding of Gestalt therapy, this is essential reading for all psychotherapists and anyone seeking to understanding how we exist as human beings and as part of a plurality of affiliations and non-affiliations.

Michela Gecele is an MD, Psychiatrist, and Gestalt psychotherapist. She formerly coordinated, in Turin, a psychological and psychiatric service for immigrants. She is an international trainer and supervisor, co-director of the International Institute of Gestalt Therapy and Psychopathology (IPSIG) and of the Turin School of Psychopathology, and co-founder of the International Study Group on Emergent Self and Field Theory (IG-FEST).

Field Perspectives and Clinical Practice: Gestalt Therapy Book Series

This series intends to make a contribution to developing an understanding of human suffering in radically relational and field terms and to promoting the development of psychopathological perspectives building on the foundations of phenomenology and Gestalt Therapy.

Here we are referring to a way of considering psychopathology simply as the set and differentiation of the forms of suffering on a relational, personal, and social level. Forms that already have within themselves a creative adaptation to vital and contextual situations, together with a meaning and a direction, even a potential.

This perspective considers suffering not as a deviation but as an expression of being human and of its oscillations in the dimensions of presence and absence.

Suffering, from this perspective, is a voice that in itself speaks to us of the support it requires and of which absence calls out for which presence, whose meanings are incessantly anchored to the world-of-life and to emerging backgrounds of meaning, whether biographical, existential, transgenerational, social, cultural, and even ecological and political.

As a basic premise of this phenomenological understanding, every aspect of life deserves to be explored, simply as potential to be supported or as a consequence, a risk, a resource, a foundation of human suffering. Whether alive or frozen, pulsating or waiting to be awakened, it is always on the move, to be transformed creatively into an encounter and natural growth.

This series aims, therefore, to support the development of a therapeutic and psychiatric clinical practice that is open to complexity, to grasp the novelty and uniqueness in every authentic encounter—including those with other disciplines—and capable of tolerating the unknown without sheltering behind facile and often iatrogenic simplifications. The therapeutic approach developed in this series seeks to be embodied and experiential, but also strongly anchored to theory and inspired by continuous critical reflection.

The series offers a background that supports clinicians in questioning themselves in each and every therapeutic encounter, which presupposes and contributes to the responsible co-creation of our world.

Gianni Francesetti, Michela Gecele, Jan Roubal

Otherness in a Fragmented World
Psychotherapy in Contemporary Society
Michela Gecele

Otherness in a Fragmented World
Psychotherapy in Contemporary Society

Michela Gecele

Routledge
Taylor & Francis Group
LONDON AND NEW YORK

Designed cover image: Focus Cover 40

First published 2025
by Routledge
4 Park Square, Milton Park, Abingdon, Oxon OX14 4RN

and by Routledge
605 Third Avenue, New York, NY 10158

Routledge is an imprint of the Taylor & Francis Group, an informa business

© 2025 Michela Gecele

The right of Michela Gecele to be identified as author[/s] of this work has been asserted in accordance with sections 77 and 78 of the Copyright, Designs and Patents Act 1988.

All rights reserved. No part of this book may be reprinted or reproduced or utilised in any form or by any electronic, mechanical, or other means, now known or hereafter invented, including photocopying and recording, or in any information storage or retrieval system, without permission in writing from the publishers.

Trademark notice: Product or corporate names may be trademarks or registered trademarks and are used only for identification and explanation without intent to infringe.

First Italian Edition published by Giovanni Fioriti Editore 2021

Gli sfondi dell'alterita:

La terapia della Gestalt nell'orizzonte sociale e culturale: tra frammentazione e

globalizzazione

di Michela Gecele

Copyright© 2021 Giovanni Fioriti Editore s.r.l.

ISBN: 978-88-3625-022-6

The English translation rights arranged through Rightol Media

(Email: copyright@rightol.com)

First English edition published by Routledge 2025

ISBN: 978-1-032-84723-8 (hbk)
ISBN: 978-1-032-93930-8 (pbk)
ISBN: 978-1-003-56829-2 (ebk)

DOI: 10.4324/9781003568292

Typeset in Times New Roman
by KnowledgeWorks Global Ltd.

Contents

Foreword to the English Edition		*vi*
LYNNE JACOBS		
Preface		*ix*
JESSICA GHIONI		
Introduction		*xii*
1	Culture as a Plurality of Maps	1
2	'Cultivating Humanity': Intercultural Training	6
3	Otherness, Othernesses	13
4	Invisible Grounds	26
5	Narrating, Communicating, and Translating	44
6	Linguistic Grounds: Bringing Reality to Life	51
7	Novelty, Familiarity, Support: Relational Intentionality in Creative Adjustment	65
	Hunger and Doubt: Afterword	*75*
	FRANCESCO REMOTTI	
	Index	*83*

Foreword to the English Edition
Lynne Jacobs

Much of the writing of Gestalt therapists that emerges from Europe carries the density and heft of its long, long history, even if mostly by implication. I think this is especially true of the writings of Italian gestalt therapists, whose bodies and built environments are saturated with the histories and the myths and legends that have shaped their culture and the culture of psychotherapy. The history, myths, and legends are like a shadow that moves in the background, hovering under their words, whispering, "There is more here than my written words can convey. Let your ground subtly speak to you from its shadows. Let your body, your feelings, your intuitions resonate as you read my paltry words."

As I have said many times, European gestalt therapy and theory is also a hotbed of creative, expansive new theorizing and therapeutic practice, much (but not all) of it coming from Italy. This book is another creative entry. On the one hand, this book is easy to read, clearly laid out in sections and subsections that expose what we mean by contacting from a variety of angles. On the other, it is disquieting in its focus on the inevitable disruptiveness of the necessary decentring that dialogic contacting requires.

I resonate with Ghioni's preface, in which she describes the difficulties and enrichments that Gecele's journey beckons us to take together:

> A journey that, if we undertake it prepared to be disoriented and with a good dose of patience in finding ourselves again, both the same and different, can be truly transformative, just as every journey is when worthy of such a name.

That description fits my experience while I read Gecele's words. Gecele's explorations get to the foundations of what it means to be a 'human among humans,' and also inextricably 'of a world.' The journey Ghioni mentions is recursive. The themes repeat, but the journey is a spiralling circle. I notice as I move through my life, engage in dialogue, struggle to find my bearings, I often find myself thinking, "This is what Gecele means!"

Gecele uses the current Italian experience with mass migration to try to understand what we are pulled to do when we meet a foreigner, the 'other,' and what we must do to truly find them, and to find ourselves as well. If we cannot welcome the foreign other, the stranger to whom we are also other, we are all diminished.

Importantly, Gecele describes intentions and processes that are invaluable for us as therapists, but this is not solely a book about therapy. It is a challenge to us, as our national and cultural borders become more porous, more intermixed, to dare to surrender to the deeper challenges that contacting has become. And with each surrender, difficult may it be, we find the other more fully, only by re-finding and reconfiguring, our own more expanded selves. I felt challenged, not only as a therapist, but as a citizen, as well.

Gecele's book is a political manifesto (in the best sense of the word, 'political'). It is also psychological, focused primarily on exploring what contacting is, in its most radical interhuman sense. She describes throughout the paradox of finding the other, and by do so, finding one's self. But this only can occur if you are willing to start the journey by momentarily relinquishing your ideas about yourself and instead submit to how you are seen by the other, including how, like it or not, you represent a community, a group, a worldview. And at the same time, we must keep in mind that the other is always more than we can know, since, becoming is always occurring, and also our own parameters, perspectives, our situatedness in and of a context, can never be all-encompassing. Thus, Polster's love of curiosity is more relevant now than ever, in that we cannot really ultimately know the other, but we can perhaps revel in their otherness, and perhaps expand our own experiential horizons while we meet their complexity, our being towards the moment, our intermingling next emergence of selfhood and new community.

Here is an example of the ground she lays out early in the book, as she maps our journey:

> One way of decentralizing our point of view and truly experiencing the plurality of perspectives and human forms is to reflect on how others see us—not as individuals, but as a group, community, or society.
>
> (p.26)

It is important to start, each and every time, by listening, because words can take on different meanings, just as emotions, mindsets, and life experiences can. We need to prepare ourselves to truly listen and, at the same time, find the right words to explain ourselves.

(p.36)

> Every approach to experience, every theoretical perspective in psychotherapy, just like in other disciplines, derives from a specific point of view, from a precise position in space-time. One's positioning in a context, in a framework of roles and affiliations, inevitably becomes the centre from which other positions and experiences are measured and described as close or distant, as more or less accordant, compatible, *and corresponding with a norm.*
>
> (my Italics, p.46)

Gecele takes the reader through recursive loops as she explores meeting the other, especially, but not only, the immigrant other. But each loop begins at a different point, a different emergence from the ground process of developing good coordination with ever-moving figure/ground processes. With each iteration, she complexifies and enriches just what we mean by skilful contact, and one's skilful figure/ground process as the key to meaningful living.

She takes the readers through different pathways along the figure/ground contacting processes that she avers are necessary for the health of all (and, I believe, including our non-human environment). In each chapter she quotes liberally from other authors, and I, for one, am grateful that she did so, so that I can get a taste of what those who are writing in other languages are saying. She never says that the kind of dialogue she advocates is easy. And as I read her book, I was disquieted many times, while at the same time agreeing with her statements. I had the sense of trying to keep my balance while standing on a boat in rocky waves.

A very important perspective she reiterates in various ways is to remember that the figure always implies a ground, and it is our receptivity to the ground that makes what Buber might call a 'genuine encounter' possible. We can listen for the subliminal clues of ground—and Gecele is showing us how to do so—and we must remain humble about how our ground may be more visible (figural) to the other. Thus, it is through listening with a dialogical attitude that one may find one's self through the eyes of the other, while simultaneously, they are revealed to themselves through your eyes. In good conversation, built on curiosity and respectful listening, the figures flow, one after another, allowing the depth of the ground to be revealed and to shape a next moment.

Gecele calls on us to have the humility and the courage to dwell with the ground. This means slowing down when listening, not cycling quickly from one figure to another. Trust that over time one develops the felt sense of a richness, solidity, a sense that this figure comes from a ground, and is pointing as much to the ground as it is to its vivid 'figuralness.' A sense that the ground that supports the figure is something to 'let be known.' It can be a ground that, by sensing it, gives rise to a near—and hopefully more refined figure, as the figure ground process is able to move along in a coordinated, rather than fragmented way.

And then, we can stand in and on the grounds of otherness.

Preface
Jessica Ghioni

This book opens with the suggestive image of the journey as a metaphor of life. From there we are led on an out-and-out journey through *the grounds of otherness*, on a trail exploring the individual and collective terrains, or grounds, from which figures of otherness—the various forms othernesses take—emerge. A journey that, if we undertake it prepared to be disoriented and with a good dose of patience in finding ourselves again, both the same and different, can be truly transformative, just as every journey is when worthy of such a name. Thus, we wander from an exploration of the concept of culture, of the tools suited to working with it as care workers and social workers, of language, migration, and art, to observing the horizons of otherness, to then ultimately discover othernesses in every relationship, encounter, and breath of life.

Reading this book by Michela Gecele is therefore an experience. By this I mean that every paragraph engages us in a true experience, allowing us to enjoy its treasures and go through its difficulties. To sweep through the sensations and thoughts that emerge, to dive in and then re-emerge with the sense of an expanded horizon and a new fullness in contact. In this experience, I brought (brought back) to life the *grounds of otherness* I have constructed over the years, living and growing between different worlds and languages, both as a person and a professional.

In exploring the themes of this book, the author draws support from Gestalt therapy and its language as a map for orienting her way in understanding relationships and forms of social and political cohabitation. It is a theory that, besides placing fundamental importance on contexts, on the 'loci' of growth and encounter between individuals, proposes a somewhat 'organic' approach to the constituent processes of the self. As such, in addressing the functions of the self it talks about contacts that nourish, about chewing novelty, swallowing and digesting it. This theoretical ground is perhaps part of the reason why an image stuck with me throughout my reading the book—the image of a banquet. A sumptuous banquet with an 'Asian flavour,' where the various dishes are served all together on the same table. It brings to mind the films *Eat Drink Man Woman* (Taiwan 1994) and *The Farewell* (USA/China 2019), in which human affairs and cultural grounds intertwine, clashing with each other and enriching each other mutually, just like the carefully prepared dishes that accompany the lives of the characters. That is the way 'the banquet' of *The Grounds of Otherness* is savoured, where every dish—every chapter—reveals unexpected flavours on first bite. Considerations emerge from the ground; the surprise of the taste and colour grows with the second mouthful. Each chapter is a miniature world in itself, an experience of otherness that needs to be taken in slowly, connected with one's own experiences, sensations, memories, songs, and films. It is not a book to be devoured from cover to cover, but nibbled on slowly, going back perhaps to chew again on a morsel to improve its digestion and assimilation. When it comes to otherness, there are so many worlds in one world, almost like a pop-up book. As the author writes at the end of the book, "This is one of the possible conclusions to our journey. There could be many others. Or perhaps there is no conclusion, but just rests, moments of possible assimilation. To then set off again and come face-to-face with familiarity and novelty, just as in life."

In the text, implicit grounds are made explicit, brought to light and nourished by it, to then return to being grounds, enriched and renewed. Every chapter opens up new possibilities for insight, sparking in us a desire to re-read books we already know under a new light, to be guided by cultural anthropology in understanding events, or to make use of concepts from Chinese Medicine. The reader receives incessant cues to continue learning, discovering, and growing. For example, re-reading the passage from Orhan Pamuk cited in the book—where the Turkish writer tells of discovering new aspects of his city, Istanbul, through the accounts of Foreigners and the eyes of Others—I surprised myself in thinking back to the experience elicited in me when reading the article "The Unlikely Triumph of Italian Nationhood" in *Internazionale*, No. 1372/2020.[1] In it, reporter Roger Cohen described the Italian summer in the time of Covid-19, when holiday-makers would stroll along the seafront with face masks hanging off their elbows or their ears. It is an image we know well, but for the first time the description moved me to feel a tenderness and a sense of affinity for an 'Italianness' which I have never believed I reflect, leading me to make peace with an identity I rejected. Michela Gecele herself underlines how, "In making this journey towards the foreigner [...] we increasingly come to realise that what we are finding are also new insights into othernesses much closer to us, keys unlocking landscapes we thought we already knew. Focusing on more macroscopic differences can help us explore the prejudices and foreknowledge that conditions our daily life experience."

This book is also, therefore, an excellent antidote against racism. It leads us to think about how reality is constructed, to observe how it is perceived and transmitted. It discloses the mechanisms of cultural rigidities, stereotypes, and prejudices. It shows us how power imbalances are forged between cultures, how collective illusions and distortions arise concerning belonging, memory, and the meaning of the world. But what works particularly well in this book is the way the author proceeds, opening up Russian dolls of thought, uncovering sentence after sentence, unpacking arguments to lead us, in a purely descriptive way, to an unexpected complexity that ultimately sheds light on a new horizon of meaning. And in the total absence of judgement. Borrowing the language used by Lucien Hounkpatin,[2] the author makes use of the complexification of the themes addressed to describe them and explain them—complexifying to resolve problems, just like the foundational god did in Hounkpatin's mythological account. "Complexify, to gather the substance of the considerations" (Hounkpatin 2002, p. 51). As Gecele explains the concept: "Dwelling in the present with awareness also means complexifying."

Thus all that remains is to encourage readers to enjoy the journey in full, to be enriched by the experience, and to savour this book through and through!

Notes

1 Originally published in *The New York Times*, August 14, 2020.
2 Psychologist and psychotherapist, Director of the Georges Devereux Centre in Paris, and lecturer at the University of Paris 8.

References

Hounkpatin L. (2002). "Identità nascoste, identità svelate." In M. Gecele (ed.) *Fra saperi ed esperienza. Interrogare identità, appartenenze e confini.* Turin: Il leone verde, pp. 49–57.

Introduction

> All organic creatures strive to stabilize their surroundings, all their changeability is a striving for self-preservation without change in a world that is liable to change and contrary to their interests; for man the changeability of his surroundings is a normal condition of living; for him the norm is life within changing conditions, *a change in the way of life*. It is no accident that from the point of view of nature man appears as a destroyer. But it is precisely *culture*, in the broad sense, that distinguishes human society from nonhuman societies. Thus it follows that dynamism is not an outer quality of culture imposed on it by the arbitrariness of external causes but is inseparable from it.
>
> (Lotman & Uspensky 1978, p. 223)

> Through the great mobilization of the modern age [...] the foreign has lost its exotic and astonishing character, but it has also become ubiquitous. The presence of foreigners has become the norm. This has required a major re-conceptual effort, not just on the part of foreigners, but also by the indigenous population. [...] The provocation and violence inherent in that should not be underestimated. Through their simple presence, foreigners compel the local population to relativize their value system, which, from that moment on, can no longer go unquestioned and be considered without rival. Locals "actively" experience their relativity, the relativity of the world they formerly considered the only one within their grasp.
>
> (La Cecla 2003, p. 55, my translation)

The metaphor of life as a journey is one of the most fertile and touching pictures for describing human experience. Journeying with openness and engagement is a way of going beyond one's boundaries, beyond what is known, a way of learning and listening. And it is with the intention of listening that we will now venture on a journey marked by encounters, affinities, experiences of disorientation, ways of being inside or outside the specific ways of dwelling in the world that we call culture.

When dealing with issues defined by keywords such as culture, belonging, systems of care, new, tradition, and society, the underlying question is whether our standard theoretical models have universal value, or whether they need to be redefined, shaped, and contextualized. In an age caught, from both a geographical point of view and the perspective of collective experience, between globalization and fragmentation, it may appear obvious to reject any possibility for universal models to exist. Yet, perhaps it is in their continuous transformation that models can be generalized. The importance of using a map to follow a path does not exclude the possibility of modifying the map itself along the way. Here we will be using a map in a more evident way at times, while keeping it folded away at others.

The epistemological assumptions of humanistic psychotherapies—Gestalt therapy in particular—and phenomenology will be used here as maps for interpreting relationships, ways of living together, and political and social domains today. In turn, these thematic areas, and the interconnected spheres of knowledge that study and shape them, can open up new possibilities and new tools in clinical work, therapist training, and the construction of psychosocial initiatives.

This journey is addressed to therapists of all schools, to care professionals, to education and social workers, and even to policymakers.

Global social processes, such as mass migration and the multiple interconnections between people and populations, have thrust society more forcefully into therapy and care settings, along with its rules, values, affiliations, and fragmentations. The process, however, is reciprocal, or rather, circular—the world steps into the therapeutic relationship and the therapeutic relationship steps out into the world. The dual relationship and the macrocontext intersect each other (Arendt 1968). Being in a relationship—any relationship—in a fully engaged way opens up a microcosm connected to the macrocosm. In therapy work, relational intentionality leads us towards both the individual and the social at the same time.

In the early days of psychoanalysis, the junction between society and psychology was built into the concept of the super-ego, an agent internal to the individual psyche, but derived and mediated by family upbringing. On that view, the family was the medium of a social order considered so static and necessary as to be 'biologized' in the Oedipal theory and in the need for the ego to keep the id in check. Today, that biological-psychoanalytic model has changed, as have the social structures and the view of the world and humankind that had contributed to producing them. In approaching any encounter, any relationship, we move onto unknown ground, a ground that has yet to exist perhaps, and contribute to creating reality, the world, and life. It is only by being citizens of our space-time that we can remain engaged and connected with each other, by grasping the uniqueness of 'that' story and 'that' encounter. That is why for us therapists it is so important to know about 'worldly things' and to use of our knowledge to interpret them, experience them, and incorporate them into a broader and multi-faceted pool of competencies.

Taking these as our premises, here we will explore the occasions and the wounds opened up by the encounter with the other—the changes, losses, possibilities, and potentialities it implies. We will speak of the lengthy journey it takes to reach the possibility of contact and presence, and the renascence that is continuously offered by exploring different contexts and fields. We will speak of the hurdles that can appear along the way and of what can support us in going beyond the Pillars of Hercules of our lives.

We will speak of otherness and, therefore, of what are called cultural differences—vessels of variable capacity in which we can situate macroscopic aspects but also imperceptible nuances, conventional commonplaces, and unexpected surprises. It may sound like a paradox, but it is precisely the common and shared experience of otherness, of being 'other' to every person or living being, that unites all human beings. For our humanity also lies in our being diverse, particular, in our being able to be so and in our being able to talk about it. Our continuous engagement in multiple interactions is a premise, and not an accessory, for our very existence.

Let me now explain the title of this book. The concept of ground, inseparable from that of figure, comes from theories of perception developed in the early twentieth century. Those theories are well exemplified by Gestalt psychology, which treats perception as a superordinate phenomenon, as a whole that transcends the sum of its parts. Perception is an immediate process that is tied to the present situation, but which is also influenced by past experiences, which form the ground of the experience taking shape. Different sets of elements can emerge from the same ground, connected by a logic of resemblance, or proximity, or continuity.

Just as perception brings together visual elements into a complete figure that stands out and differentiates itself from a ground that remains indistinct, or even fades away completely, the same happens in all our experiences—in a conversation, a lecture or a conference, when making a joke, reading a book, savouring a dish, or having an argument. We talk about one thing, presupposing and taking others for granted. We follow a line of reasoning, silencing the background noise of thousands of other thoughts. We perform an action, and in doing so bar all the other actions possible.

The idea that guides this book is that in our time, it is fundamental and vital to take a step back and delve deeper into grounds, into the implicit, into all that is taken for granted in life, just as in therapy.

References

Arendt H. (1968). *Men in Dark Times*. San Diego: Harcourt Brace & Company.
La Cecla F. (2003). *Il malinteso. Antropologia dell'incontro*. Rome/Bari: Laterza.
Lotman Yu. M., Uspensky B.A. (1978). "On the Semiotic Mechanism of Culture," translated by George Mihaychuk. *New Literary History, Vol. 9 No. 2 Soviet Semiotics and Criticism: An Anthology* (Winter 1978), pp. 211–232

1 Culture as a Plurality of Maps

The concept of culture …

If culture were eliminated, humanity would not exist. Even just the partial disintegration of this manifold legacy generates a disorientation (Mead 1967; Jourdan 2010; Remotti 2019) that can lead to confusion and violence. If we turn our focus onto extreme situations, such as the tragedy of the Rwandan genocide (Remotti 2013), we find ourselves faced with a complete and total uprooting, with situations deprived entirely of their own vision of humankind and of humanity.

> Friends,/we do not claim to comprehend/exactly why,/on the green hills of Rwanda/children of Gihanga [the founding hero of the kingdom] chopped to pieces/other children of Gihanga./But we believe we understand this:/ tear out to the root, for a whole century/the culture of a people,/and with the same fierceness you will plant, in every mind/the seeds of the crime.
> (Chant of the Dead, in Calbi 2004, p. 115, my translation)

In a more moderate way, holes and gaps in culture generate fragmentation and a lack of ground, which is what we will be looking at in this book.

Cultivating culture means cultivating humanity—in all its myriad, multifaceted aspects. Aspects that with globalization have come to permeate each other with greater speed and continuity than in the past, without, however, disappearing. 'Cultivating humanity' is a reference to Seneca,[1] and it is also the title of a book by Martha Nussbaum (1997),[2] in which she invites us to challenge differences, habits, traditions, and stereotypes, and return to classical culture to become citizens of the world; not by denying our affiliations but by working through them and deciphering them.

As impossible as it may be to broaden our experience to the point of encompassing all the human points of view and possibilities found in the world, it is nevertheless important to work on acquiring tools to help us break through—not break down—barriers and boundaries.

But what is the definition of 'culture'? Any attempt to define the term draws us onto complex and composite ground from which multiform and multifaceted

DOI: 10.4324/9781003568292-1

aspects emerge at different times to take on outlines and become figure. Considering this plurality of forms and accents given to one and the same word, let's look at a few definitions that have been put forward, reflecting perspectives that are closely connected with contemporary issues and interests.

> As collective systems of meaning, cultures belong primarily to social relationships and to networks of such relationships. Only indirectly, and without logical necessity, do they belong to places.
>
> (Hannerz 1992, p. 39)

> Culture is a historically transmitted pattern of meanings embodied in symbols, a system of inherited conceptions expressed in symbolic forms, by means of which men communicate, perpetuate, and develop their knowledge about and attitudes toward life.
>
> (Geertz 1973, p. 89)

> Culture has become a ubiquitous synonym for identity, an identity marker and differentiator.
>
> (Benhabib 2002, p. 1)

The concept of identity is continuously interlinked—in thinking, in theories, and in experience—with that of culture, at times deforming it or pinning it down.

> Identity belongs (if its use really can be found) to the level of social representations, insofar as it is a formidable ideological means of stabilization. That does not, however, mean it must necessarily be a part of the toolbox of those who intend to study them. What social agents plan and seek to fulfil is one thing; the tools that anthropologists and social scientists adopt for the purpose of study are another. [...] Anthropologists and sociologists, however, come up against the identity claims and demands of the groups they study, and this has led them to the conclusion that identities are "constructed," "imagined," "invented." [...] Identity is not a means of explaining (an explanans), and so it should not be considered part of the toolbox; rather, it is something to be explained, analysed, or described (an explanandum). [...] The theory we wish [...] to propose is that identity is not just something constructed, but it is, more precisely, something "fake." Identity—as we argued earlier (cf. §2)—is indeed a substance, but it is, more specifically, a fake and illusory substance. Identity is nothing more than the fiction or illusion of a substance.
>
> (Remotti 2010, pp. 117–119, my translation)

… and how culture intersects humanistic therapies

According to the Gestalt therapy model, the self is a boundary phenomenon and, as such, it concerns not just the individual, but the entire experience, feeling, actions, the process unfolding, together with the outcome of the process itself and the definition of its memory and meaning. The narrative of the self unfolds through the successiveness and contemporaneousness of experiences and shared moments that are inscribed in life stories and active in the here and now. It is a self that does not define any form of identity. On the contrary, it discloses relational intentionality, a drive towards what is outside the self, the awareness of an irreducible otherness that is found a priori in existence, the engine and direction for all encounters, knowledge, change, and development. It is a self that lies close both to the pre-Renaissance worldview, which did not place the individual at the centre of everything, and to post-modernity.

Just like the self in this conception of it, culture is a process. It is the continuous encounter/clash with diversity and the transformation that ensues from that. It is both the codification and store of past experiences, and the assimilation of novelty and change. It is shaped by history, by knowledge, by life events, by memory—and by all those representations and fictions that make up and define social structures. Culture is created in every encounter. It is renegotiated, redefined, and recreated in every experience of contact involving at least two people with different cultural grounds. No encounter can be an exception to such a definition!

Culture is created at the boundary, at borders, on the margins—and there are many margins in the world that often have little voice. In dealing with culture, to be a part of it, it is important to understand it, to try and transform its obligations and limitations, especially those that are unexplored, through a process of awareness and assimilation. That means choosing what to accept, what to reject, what to negotiate, starting from all of what we take for granted, having internalized it uncritically in the early stages of development, together with our mother tongue. It means understanding what is hard to give up because it is so intrinsic to the construction of our self-image.

As therapists, we can be—perhaps should be—at one and the same time, both at the centre and on the margins of our multiple cultural affiliations. We can try to use words and definitions not only as concepts internal to a culture, but also as borderline elements that upset the established order and create hybrids. Because even the upsetting of order is part of the equilibrium of things—it is ceaselessly part of the internal dynamics of a society and of intercultural relationships.

While speaking of culture, we refer not just to different places and spatial coordinates, but to temporal processes as well. We link up to history and so to stratifications of meaning, to the dynamics of power, to codifications of views of the self and of the other.

> We understand culture as the nonhereditary memory of the community, a memory expressing itself in a system of constraints and prescriptions. [...] Furthermore, insofar as culture is memory or, in other words, a record in the memory of what the community has experienced, it is, of necessity, connected to past historical experience. Consequently, at the moment of its appearance, culture cannot be recorded as such, for it is only perceived ex post facto. When people speak of the creation of a new culture, they are inevitably looking

ahead; that is, they have in mind that which (they presume) will become a memory from the point of view of the reconstructable future (of course, the correctness of such an assumption will only be shown by the future itself). [...]

It is worth recalling that one of the sharpest forms of social struggle in the sphere of culture is the obligatory demand to forget certain aspects of historical experience. Epochs of historical regression [...] in forcing upon the community highly mythologized schemes of history, end by demanding from society that it forget those texts which do not lend themselves to being so organized.

(Lotman & Uspensky 1978, p. 214, 216–17)

Or we could say, in what is an apparent contradiction, that culture is the snapshot of an instant and that in speaking of it we refer to something that no longer exists. For the moment we do, we already find ourselves in a subsequent instant, in which the infinite elements at play have already assumed a different form—like in a kaleidoscope, in which the possible images are infinite.

Notes

1 "*Iam istum spiritum expuemus. Interim, dum trahimus, dum inter hominess sumus, colamus humanitatem*", says Seneca in *De Ira* (III, 43, 5) ["Any time now, we'll cough up our last breath. For now, while we breathe and are among our fellow humans, let's cherish the qualities that make us human", translated by Robert A. Kaster and Martha C. Nussbaum in Seneca 2010, p. 96]. Martha Nussbaum stresses this aspect of "*colamus humanitatem*," choosing it for the title of her book.
2 Nussbaum is an American philosopher, Professor of Law and Ethics at the University of Chicago, and a leading voice on the international progressive stage. Her books include *The Fragility of Goodness. Luck and Ethics in Greek Tragedy and Philosophy* (Cambridge: Cambridge University Press, 1986), *Not for Profit. Why Democracy Needs the Humanities* (Princeton, NJ: Princeton University Press, 2010), and *Creating Capabilities. The Human Development Approach* (Cambridge, MA: The Belknap Press of Harvard University Press, 2011).

References

Benhabib S. (2002). *The Claims of Culture. Equality and Diversity in the Global Era*. Princeton/Oxford: Princeton University Press. Translated in Italian as *Le rivendicazioni dell'identità culturale*. Bologna: Il Mulino, 2002.

Calbi A. (ed.) (2004). *Rwanda 94. Italy for Rwanda 1994–2004*. Milan: Grafiche Granata.

Geertz C. (1973). *The Interpretation of Cultures*. New York: Basic Books. Translated in Italian as *Interpretazione di culture*. Bologna: Il Mulino, 1998.

Hannerz U. (1992). *Cultural Complexity. Studies in the Social Organization of Meaning*. New York: Columbia University Press. Translated in Italian as *La complessità culturale*. Bologna: Il Mulino, 1992.

Jourdan L. (2010). *Generazione Kalashnikow*. Rome/Bari: Laterza.

Lotman Yu. M., Uspensky B.A. (1978). "On the Semiotic Mechanism of Culture," translated by George Mihaychuk. *New Literary History, Vol. 9 No. 2 Soviet Semiotics and Criticism: An Anthology* (Winter 1978), pp. 211–232.

Mead M. (1967). *Male and Female: A Study of the Sexes in a Changing World*. New York: William Morrow.

Nussbaum M. (1997) *Cultivating Humanity. A Classical Defence of Reform in Liberal Education*. Cambridge, M.A./London: Harvard University Press. Translated in Italian as *Coltivare l'umanità. I classici, il multiculturalismo, l'educazione contemporanea*. Rome: Carocci, 2006.

Remotti F. (2010). *L'ossessione identitaria*. Rome/Bari: Laterza.

Remotti F. (2013). *Fare umanità. I drammi dell'antropo-poiesi*. Rome/Bari: Laterza.

Remotti F. (2019). *Cultura. Dalla complessità all'impoverimento*. Rome/Bari: Laterza.

Seneca L.A. (2000). *L'Ira (traduzione e introduzione di Costantino Ricci)*. Milan: Biblioteca Universale Rizzoli.

Seneca L.A. (2010) *Anger, Mercy, Revenge*. Translated by Robert A. Kaster and Martha C. Nussbaum. Chicago: The University of Chicago Press.

2 'Cultivating Humanity'
Intercultural Training

A small exercise

In the 1950s, the American anthropologist Horace Miner studied and described a population known as the Nacirema.[1] As a social group of interest for our discussion here, let's take a look at his description of them.

> The fundamental belief underlying the whole system appears to be that the human body is ugly and that its natural tendency is to debility and disease. Incarcerated in such a body, man's only hope is to avert these characteristics through the use of the powerful influences of ritual and ceremony. Every household has one or more shrines devoted to this purpose. [...]

> The focal point of the shrine is a box or chest which is built into the wall. In this chest are kept the many charms and magical potions without which no native believes he could live. These preparations are secured from a variety of specialized practitioners. The most powerful of these are the medicine men, whose assistance must be rewarded with substantial gifts. However, the medicine men do not provide the curative potions for their clients, but decide what the ingredients should be and then write them down in an ancient and secret language. This writing is understood only by the medicine men and the herbalists who, for another gift, provide the required charms. [...]

> The Nacirema have an almost pathological horror and fascination with the mouth, the condition of which is believed to have a supernatural influence on all social relationships. Were it not for the rituals of the mouth, they believe that their teeth would fall out, their gums bleed, their jaws shrink, their favorite friends desert them and their lovers reject them. They also believe that a strong relationship exists between oral and moral characteristics. For example, there is a ritual ablution of the mouth for children which is supposed to improve their moral fiber.

> The daily body ritual performed by everyone includes a mouth rite. Despite the fact that these people are so punctilious about the care of the

DOI: 10.4324/9781003568292-2

mouth, this rite involves a practice which strikes the uninitiated stranger as revolting. It was reported to me that the ritual consists of inserting a small bundle of hog hairs into the mouth, along with certain magical powders, and them moving the bundle in a highly formalized series of gestures.

(Miner 1956, pp. 503–504)

Why have we reported this description here? Because it is a small exercise for us to do together, by answering a few simple questions. Who might this population be? One distant from us or close to us? Do they remind us of other social groups we know? In which part of the world do, or did, the Nacirema live?

Think about it and then stop for a moment, imagining a blank page in the text. Now, let's read the word 'Nacirema' backwards.[2]

Lots of tools have been constructed to help us shift, if only for an instant, our point of view and observe the ideology and structure of the world we live in from the outside in. Rarely do they fail to achieve their desired effect. However, the stronger the astonishment provoked, the more attention needs to be focused on the process of integrating and assimilating new experiences into our values, thoughts, views, and habits—so that the surprise of an instant can become a starting point for truly calling into question prejudices. "The objective of the intercultural workshops is, generally, to astonish people, to render cultural prejudices and their relative limits explicit, and to bring about an experience that is truly changing" (Gecele 2008, p. 180, my translation). The initial astonishment proves all the more effective and transformative the more there is a willingness to grasp and welcome novelty. It is instead harder to question one's beliefs when fear and insecurity are present and widespread, at the individual, family, and social levels.

Under the eye of others

One way of decentralizing our point of view and truly experiencing the plurality of perspectives and human forms is to reflect on how others see us—not as individuals, but as a group, community, or society. Many papers and research studies call forth and describe the eye of 'the other' as the bearer of another culture. In them we find distant experiences, astonishing points of view, words we do not identify with and that we find surprising, but also expressions that lie close to our way of thinking and speaking, but which are striking because they are uttered not by us but by others. The quotes that follow give a few examples.[3]

> Italians are curious; they are people who, if you approach them, when you ask for information, even if they do not know they give you the information all the same.
>
> (Bruno Ventre 1994, p. 52, my translation)

Whatever you do, Italians always thank you.

(Ibid.)

What I like about Italians is their friendliness. They laugh even if they hurt you; they put on a nice face and I like that.

(Ibid., p. 54)

Italians in general like working; others are instead very good at faking it.

(Ibid., p. 55)

After having walked across all of Bologna, I have come to the surprising conclusion that anyone without money cannot live.

(Diawnè 1989, p. 71, my translation)

From a Chinese point of view, it can be said that Italy lacks an ideology shared across the nation, which can act as an internal force of cohesion.

(Wang 1989, p. 190, my translation)

If two important men (Falcone and Borsellino) can be killed just like that, think of what they can do to us. Judge Falcone often loved to say: "For me as a Sicilian, my life is worth as much as a button." And for me as an African, how much can my life be worth in Italy?"

(Sangiorgi 1995, p. 72, my translation)

Even making a sale is depressing, when you realise the buyer is driven solely by compassion, that your eagles and elephants are barely of interest, that only the generosity of others allows you to survive. Let's hope things change. For now, ours is a life of humiliation.

(Khouma 1990, p. 91, my translation)

The dialogues that follow are taken from a research project promoted by the 'Beyond Racism Committee' of Turin (Borello et al. 2008), carried out in schools and other places where young people hang out. The objective was to promote thinking on the topics of living together and citizenship, with focus groups used as the main research tool. Quoted here are the words of young people of varying degrees of 'Italianness.'

El:[4] "My vote won't change anything anyway. It's just a waste of time."
R:[5] "Yeah, but if everybody says that …"
El: "I've been here for fifteen years and I still have to renew my residence permit."
Ca:[6] "It's so expensive and such a hassle for the documents. They want thousands of photos and they're always taking your fingerprints … I mean, it's always me! And then they make a mess of your hands and it takes a week for it to go away."

El:	"It's true, a cross doesn't belong in a classroom. The cross belongs in church."
En:[7]	"Yeah, but ultimately the council's Christian ... I don't know, it shouldn't bother anyone."
El:	"In my view, it doesn't make sense, it's not like you pray in class. It belongs in church, or at home. And then, not everybody's Christian."
S:[8]	"I agree in a way, but not entirely. I mean, in the end you're in Italy, people are Christian, and you're an outsider. But they're the ones who should understand it should go. Anyway, it doesn't bother me at all."
Y:[9]	"In China, they're all Buddhist, but there's no Buddha at school!"
S:	"Yeah, because people don't know anything, they just hear what they say on TV. I mean ... what's banned for us makes sense, because even the veil signifies identification and respect. They should go learn to know that Islam isn't a religion like it seems, where, like, some guy goes and kills his daughter because she won't wear the veil. My father might lecture me a bit, but he doesn't force me to do anything. There are others that do, but they're family issues."
Cl:[10]	"Even where I'm from, you wear a veil in church."
El:	"Even in Albania you see old women with veils, but not that many ... but then it's not as though I've ever been to church in Albania."
Cl:	"If you go scantily dressed, it's not like the priest will tell you to leave or give you a bad look, he'll humiliate you publicly, pointing you out to everyone. And you can't go in with piercings."
El:	"Even in Albania you don't see piercings."
S:	"In Morocco people have them, there's everything. I don't like the Islam you find in countries like Pakistan or Afghanistan. In Morocco it's different, because it's a free country, more or less. There's not just freedom of the press, people can do what they like. In Afghanistan, that a woman can't go out is excessive, it's a life of hell. In Morocco, it's not like that. And then the new queen has given women lots of rights."
W:[11]	"They shouldn't give citizenship to everyone, even to criminals ... only to people who deserve it."
P:[12]	"I know lots of foreigners who don't pay taxes here. Only 15 per cent pay taxes."
B:[13]	"My dad pays social security, but he won't get a full pension neither from Italy nor Albania, where he started working, because in both countries he won't have the right number of years of contributions to get it. Who thinks about them? States need to negotiate a huge number of agreements, especially where there's a high percentage of foreigners, like Albania and Italy."
F:[14]	"Loads of my relatives have gone to live in England, or in the United States, though in the USA it's much harder. Whereas it's much easier to go and live in England. To live there and even get citizenship. For

instance ... I don't know how to say it ... it doesn't matter. Anyway, there are lots of people who have gotten English citizenship, even in the past, and after only a short time. For instance, if you apply for it, if you live in Italy and apply, it takes just three months, or at most five or six, and then they give you a reply and it's almost sure they'll accept you if you're an honest person, and you work, etc. Did I say Italy? I meant England."

Grasping nuances, broadening awareness

Numerous approaches are used for training in the intercultural field, which cuts across disciplines, techniques, and schools. So far, we have mostly considered an approach that uses exercises and experiments to bring about a decentralization with respect to one's usual cultural coordinates.

Another way of working is to encourage thinking about personal experiences, fostering listening and a climate of interest.

> Starting on work with the intercultural aspect of personal experiences means concentrating on open Gestalts, on material that has not been assimilated, on the little things and big things in life, on choices, travels, movements, and changes. It is about working on awareness and on assimilation, about guiding a person in returning to what has gone unseen, to what has been paid little attention, to what has not been assimilated, perhaps because there was little support for it. Narrating and revisiting personal experience involves pausing to look at movements and encounters with the other, considering that it is through the experience of being accepted that we are transformed. It is about delving—with a microscope and in slow motion (as training in Gestalt therapy prepares us to do)—into the "little" moments of daily life, into the daily experiences of detachment, breakage, approach, and encounter. [...] It is also about rendering explicit, and sharing, the pathways that ceaselessly make us grow, together with the places and contexts that have meaning for us, including those apparently lost in time and memory.
> (Gecele 2008, pp. 183–184, my translation)

The risk that lies in notions

> The third training approach used to get to know "the other" is the in-depth exploration of the contents, cultural differences, habits, lifestyles, and mindsets of human groups that live in different latitudes to our own and that have gone through different historical stages. Such an approach is "perilous" if used on its own, as it risks "freezing" what in reality is in continuous motion and redefinition—in other words, all that we call culture.
> (Gecele 2006, p. 41, my translation)

This third approach is useful above all as a complement to the others, to avoid the risk, when used on its own, of prejudices hindering the real experience of the other, and hence encounter. By 'prejudices' we also include here 'positive' prejudices, such as the unconditional appreciation of diversity/exoticism, which is often implicit in statements of tolerance, cultural relativism, and self-descriptions of openness.

Only with true openness, produced by decentralization and awareness, can we really feel the resonances of others' experiences, without reducing them to something already known. It is in this way that we can continue to construct and produce culture, drawing also on information and knowledge from cultural anthropology and other disciplines.

Culture as art and experience

Cinema and travel experiences are ways of putting together the three training approaches mentioned here. As is literature, perhaps in even a stronger way, as it allows pauses and moments of assimilation. "Fiction is a support, a place of encounter, for recognizing and integrating parts of our lives and our experience that we have not had the chance to see, narrate, and assimilate; but it is also a place for encountering novelty—'other' experiences" (Gecele 2006, p. 41, my translation).

Notes

1 In Italian it was translated as the 'Inacirema.'
2 Of course, the exercise could be repeated through the observation of the Nailati, the Namreg, the Hsinaps, etc. by a foreigner.
3 Let me also mention, by way of example, other works of various forms and kinds: G. Sammartino, *Siamo qui. Storie e successi di donne migranti* (Rome: Bordeaux Edizioni, 2018); I. Scego, *Future. Il domani narrato dalle voci di oggi* (Florence: Effequ, 2019); M.A. Toscano (ed.) *Poesie migranti. Antologia della differenza ribelle*, Volantini militanti No. 9 (Trieste: Asterios, 2020).
4 Albanian girl, aged 17 years, educated in Italy.
5 Moroccan boy, aged 19 years, living in Italy for 10 years.
6 Romanian girl, aged 20 years, living in Italy for four years.
7 Albanian girl, aged 18 years, living in Italy for 10 years.
8 Moroccan girl, aged 17 years, born in Italy.
9 Chinese boy, aged 18 years, living in Italy for nine years.
10 Romanian girl, aged 20 years, living in Italy for five years.
11 Moroccan boy, aged 21 years, who came to Italy when he was eight years old, at a time when immigration was still a rather limited phenomenon, in terms of the numbers. He works in a coffee bar.
12 Peruvian girl, aged 22 years, studying at university to become a nurse.
13 Albanian girl, aged 20 years, living in Turin for four years and in her second year of Law. She has already gained some work experience in the field of cultural mediation.
14 Girl of Somali heritage, aged 14 years, born in Italy with Italian citizenship. She has just finished middle school.

References

Borello F., De Martini M, Ghioni J., Ricucci R., Sansoè R., Trucco D., Ciafaloni F. (eds.) (2008). *Gli adolescenti immigrati tra integrazione, differenziazione, contrapposizione*. Turin: Comitato Oltre il Razzismo.

Bruno Ventre A. (ed.) (1994). *Nato in Senegal, immigrato in Italia*. Milan: Edizione Ambiente.

Diawnè D. (1989). "Suoni e racconti di un narratore africano a Bologna." In A. Le Pichon, L. Caronia (eds.) *Sguardi venuti da lontano. Un'indagine di transcultura*. Milan: Bompiani.

Gecele M. (2006). "Narrare percorsi di vita e realtà sociali: il sostegno della letteratura." In A.M. Di Vita, V. Granatella (eds.) *Patchwork narrativi. Modelli ed esperienze tra identità e dialogo*. Milan: Edizioni Unicopli.

Gecele M. (2008). "Incontri con l'alterità. Il terapeuta della Gestalt fra il decentramento culturale e la responsabilità sociale." In A. Ferrara, M. Spagnuolo Lobb (eds.) *Le voci della Gestalt. Sviluppi e innovazioni di una psicoterapia*. Milan: FrancoAngeli.

Khouma P. (1990). *Io, venditore di elefanti. Una vita per forza fra Dakar, Parigi e Milano*. Milan: Garzanti.

Miner H. (1956). "Body Ritual Among the Nacirema." *American Anthropologist* 58, 3, 503–507.

Sangiorgi R. (ed.) (1995). *Le voci dell'arcobaleno*. Santarcangelo di Romagna: Fara Editore.

Wang B. (1989). "Il sogno italiano infestato dai fantasmi." In A. Le Pichon L. Caronia (eds.) *Sguardi venuti da lontano. Un'indagine di transcultura*. Milan: Bompiani.

3 Otherness, Othernesses

The man-woman paradigm of incompleteness

Denying the intrinsic difference in being humans, denying the relational nature implicit in the incompleteness of the individual man or woman, can be seen as a kind of original sin—a risk that is innate to humanity. When at the centre of a culture or a society there is only man, in the sense of male, this presumed completeness and univocality tends to lead to a destabilizing omnipotence.

> What is truly unthought of in the Western tradition, starting from Plato, is difference. Difference is innate in every creature—singular and unique is the difference imprinted into the flesh that makes every creature not humankind, but a creature belonging to one of two genders, to one of two sexes. Starting from metaphysics, Western history has instead constructed difference as differentiation, translating it into a form of dominion.
> (Cavarero 2007, pp. 75–76, my translation)

Here we will look at the experience of male-female diversity as paradigmatic of the incompleteness of the human being, on which a multiplicity of political and cultural constructions have become stratified over time and across space (Mead 1967; Ardener 1978; Maher 1992; Gilligan 1982, 2003; Rubin 2004).

> The true violence on which everything is founded is the universalization and claim to absoluteness of only one of the two sexes of humankind, which founds on itself civilization and the political order and begins to displace from its own centrality all differences, including, above all, sexual difference. This dynamic, or model, runs across all of Western culture, but its essential outlines can already be found in Ancient Greece. What we need to call attention to is that, whereas initially, when still in the making, this process betrayed the problematic aspects of its own construction, later everything became obvious.

Women would stay at home, men would engage in politics and war—it would all be normal. The order was taken to be obvious, just as it would be taken to be obvious that if the political order fell, all chaos would break loose.

(Cavarero 2007, pp. 40ff., my translation)

The transformation of difference into hierarchy, referred specifically here to the man-woman relationship and described and situated in a historical dimension, tells us that there is always a risk in every encounter with what is novel and diverse, in every encounter with the other. Positing, or implicitly assuming, the existence of a—value, economic, cultural—scale on which to place the representatives of humanity lays the bases for a distorted relationship with otherness.

Duality and triality

Duality is the extreme simplification of cultural, and hence human, complexity, one most laden with consequences. Duality is polarization, the defining of oneself or a person or thing as being inside or outside, for or against, be it a phenomenon, a context, values, ideas, decisions. In every instant, contraposition can transform into lack, defectiveness, subordination, or the defeat of one side with respect to the other.

Going back to the example of the man-woman relationship, it should be stressed how the incompleteness of the human being can lead to an ideal dream of completeness through perfect duality, through two becoming one, in a sort of return to a paradise lost. This opens up a variety of historical, cultural, and relational horizons—from the Platonic myth to the multiple forms given to the mother-child relationship, from folie à deux to the search for the perfect partner, able to satisfy our every need, to certain inferior forms of mysticism. Or even to the epic feats of Don Juan or the works of the Marquis de Sade.

Only if the utopia of self-sufficiency encounters a limit on its way will a painful possibility be opened up for transcendence into creative fertility. Otherwise, if it does not broaden its sights and move towards the world, Narcissus's mirror will turn on itself, becoming ever more static and deadly.

Today, more than ever, the lesson of Marguerite Duras's novels is relevant: the way—the *only* way—to have an intense and fulfilling personal (sexual) relationship is not for the couple to look into each other's eyes, forgetting about the world around them, but, while holding hands, to look together outside, at a third point (the Cause for which both are fighting, in which both are engaged).

(Žižek 2002, pp. 85–86)

Duality and its possible, or necessary, opening towards triality is a key issue in any discourse on otherness, in any discourse on relationality. Triality can be understood as the hiatus found in every interaction, as an opening towards the world and to the multiplicity of the possible, as awareness of human limit and incompleteness. To continue with the same example, power disparities in the man-woman relationship can thus be understood as a hindrance to openness, to the awareness of limit, and to the need to push forward to develop one's humanity in full. It is no coincidence that the greatest disparities—at various levels, such as in the structure of society, in the male imagination, in literature—often come paired with an ideal image of the feminine as a paradise and haven. By remaining focused on itself, duality does not establish reality, but the will. Unsurprisingly, humanization paths, whether religious or secular, involve opening up the relationship to a creator principle, a vocation, or ethical principles of social life.

Otherness, in the sense of a third point, opens up time and space, whereas fusion annuls all possibility of encounter, and hence of life. Reality—which both pre-exists the relationship and is constructed by it at the same time—slips out of the flow of time (Salonia 2004b) and loses its meaningfulness.

> Man and woman stand face-to-face in all their diversity. To be "face-to-face" is a way of saying they recognise each other reciprocally—Adam defines himself as male standing before the body of Eve; Eve defines herself as female standing before the body of Adam. Diversity lies in the recognition of one's own identity. The other should not be perceived as an extension of oneself, or as a mirror that reflects one's own image, but as diverse, as other, as someone who dwells in affective and perceptive worlds that do not conform to mine. There can be no genuine recognition of equality without a concept of "facing," of the impossibility of grasping the other. The critique of a resemblance that slides into a symbiosis that annuls differences was one of the key messages of Emmanuel Lévinas.[1] The other is in front because and inasmuch as it is Face, Face as Epiphany of the diversity of souls that in the diversity of bodies is enclosed and represented. The dream of a relationship that is nourished by "givenness" is ultimately a perspective that Bateson would call "dormitive" because it leads to fusional numbness.[2]
> (Salonia 2004a, p. 57, my translation)

The third element of a relationship can take on different forms, through to encompassing the sense and direction of the encounter, the acceptance of diversity and limit, the relationship itself, and the ground from which it originates.

Through the unknowability of the other

The question of otherness, therefore, intertwines continuously with triality, as well as with all that we can call ground. Speaking about otherness means speaking about the ground, because the figure—the moment or instant of contact, of looking each other in the eye, or in the soul, and seeing ourselves in transparency—is the moment in which othernesses encounter each other and transcend themselves. It is also the moment, perhaps, when they stand out in full.

> A going outside oneself that is addressed to the other, the stranger. It is between strangers that the encounter takes place; otherwise it would be kinship. All thought is subordinated to the ethical relation, to the infinitely other in the other person, and to the infinitely other for which I am nostalgic. Thinking the other person is a part of the irreducible concern for the other. Love is not consciousness.
>
> (Lévinas 1999, pp. 97–98)

> The idea of infinity, in which being overflows the idea, in which the other overflows the same, breaks with the inward play of the soul and alone deserves the name experience, a relationship with the exterior.
>
> (Lévinas 1987, p. 56)

The more we broaden our awareness of the ground—in the sense of what we take for granted, of what is not immediately relevant to the process underway, of what we do not comprehend or do not want to see, of what is possible, potential, in the becoming—the more we broaden our experience of being a part of humankind, with the limits that entails and with the implicitness of always being diverse and foreign.

> [...] a Jesuit missionary—was making his way to the capital when he and the story's protagonist cross paths. Their meeting therefore happens by merest accident. [...] There is an awkward, naïve quality to their conversations, initially characterized by perplexity. Given that these men come from places so distant from each other, it would have taken them time to find common ground. They listen to each other but do not, at first, hear. Partly this is a matter of language. When their discussions touch upon the nature of love, however, something changes.
>
> (Cheng 2004, p. 7).

Always a bit foreign, the 'other' brings out the grounds, the aspects that are not truly seen, lived, clarified, or shared. Perhaps many experiences and parts of our lives await an 'other' to bring them out to become present, vivid, and assimilable.

> According to Benjamin, the enthusiasm for seeing a city from the outside is the exotic or picturesque. For natives of a city, the connection is always mediated by memories.
>
> What I am describing may not, in the end, be special to Istanbul, and perhaps, with the westernization of the entire world, it is inevitable. Perhaps this is why I sometimes read Westerners' accounts not at arm's length,

as someone else's exotic dreams, but drawn close by, as if they were my own memories. I enjoy coming across a detail that I have noticed but never remarked upon, perhaps because no one else I know has either.

(Pamuk 2006, p. 240)

Our societies are swept by a sort of self-deception, a mystification that is also encouraged by the popularized distortion and simplification of psychoanalysis, which is that the other can be approached and known in its entirety— that it is not a mystery.

Just as we deny, or sugar-coat, the fact that death and suffering are part of human life, thereby reducing the possibility for sharing and finding support for those experiences, even diversity, as a foundational element of humanity, is often wiped out. The attempt to approach the other can become a step in the opposite direction, a distancing, when it appeases us, when it makes us feel that the distance can be removed completely. Rather, it is important to be aware that all we are doing is opening up a door for the difficult interaction of diverse experiences, stories, visions, and grounds. We are not resolving and flattening differences but constructing a new, fertile terrain of complexity, new pathways to follow. The vital expansion fuelled by continuous contact with otherness and the world comes to a halt when—as is often the case—the otherness is not really such but just an empty shell, a sort of myth or utopia. A place in which to situate and seek what it is we need, what it is we lack. A sort of distorted and distorting mirror which shuts off the experience instead of opening up a multitude of new possibilities.

A truth that does "not" provoke or that "only" provokes does not give us nourishment and holds back our growth. Lévinas[3] himself identified in Buber's notion of reciprocity[4] the risk of a "novelty" that assimilates the other to oneself and to one's expectations.

(Salonia 2007, p. 154, my translation)

If we do not feel we are 'other' to our interlocutor and to the world, which we nevertheless contribute to shaping and to which we give voice, and if we do not shift the focus from ourselves in situating the origin and meaning of our lives, we may well believe that our own, chronic point of view actually matches reality. That is why as therapists we constantly seek out new tools to reflect on, acquire experience of, and expand the discourse on otherness. It is important to start, each and every time, by listening, because words can take on different meanings, just as emotions, mindsets, and life experiences can. We need to prepare ourselves to truly listen and, at the same time, find the right words to explain ourselves.

A play of perspectives

Every approach to experience, every theoretical perspective in psychotherapy, just like in other disciplines, derives from a specific point of view, from a precise position in space-time. One's positioning in a context, in a framework of roles and affiliations, inevitably becomes the centre from which other positions and experiences are measured and described as close or distant, as more or less accordant, compatible, and corresponding with a norm.

Starting out from a socio-political-economic position and positing it at the centre puts into motion dynamics of power, and cultural and value domination. It is important to be aware of the risk we constantly run of falling into a 'different from' perspective. Nobody is immune to this risk. Training, knowledge levels, and artistic and intellectual talents do not shield us from beliefs, definitions, and prejudices that are widespread and shared within a social group of reference.

It is interesting to see how Orhan Pamuk describes the shifting view of Istanbul among Western intellectuals and writers, with the progressive decline of the Ottoman empire and the rise of the 'West.'

> A new generation of travelers did slowly become aware that the Ottoman Empire was crumbling, and so had little cause to wonder about the secret of the Ottoman army's success or the hidden workings of its government; instead of seeing the city as frightening and impenetrable, they came to see it as strange but amusing, a tourist attraction. [...] Having nothing of interest to say about the city, [André Gide] and his ilk were confident enough to blame their boring, featureless subject, and they made notably little effort to hide their military and economic chauvinism from more "critical" Western intellectuals. For them, the West set the standard for all humankind.
> (Pamuk 2006, pp. 237–238)

When dwelling in dominant cultural contexts, questioning the assumptions behind our every thought and perception is often a tiring process of swimming against the mainstream.

Shifting from the centre can be all the more difficult when one lives in an environment that reinforces the legitimacy of one's point of view, naturalizing one single outlook on the world, history, and life. Orhan Pamuk is a master in describing the hall of mirrors created between false alterities that reflect back to each other, between what is novel and what seems to be so, between an 'I' and a 'non-I' that permeate each other. He weaves together stories[5] that reveal the interconnections between East and West, alluding to the ever-present risk of constructing false dichotomies.

> ... the love-hate relationship with the western gaze became all the more convoluted. [...] The vicious circle is fed by westernizing intellectuals who long to hear the prominent writers and publishers of the West praise them for being like Westerners. Writers like Pierre Loti, by contrast, make no secret of loving Istanbul and the Turkish people for the opposite reason: for the preservation of their eastern particularity and their resistance to becoming western. In the days when Pierre Loti was

criticizing Istanbullus for losing touch with their traditions, he had only a small following in Turkey, most of it, ironically, among the westernizing minority.

(Pamuk 2006, p. 233)

Relationships and truth: The third as guarantor?

Every encounter with otherness that does not become an engulfment and annihilation of the other, or an experience of helplessness and impotency, implies the need to transcend ourselves by dwelling in the reality and truth of the relationship.

> Perhaps the truth that we need is always here before us in the present, in the here and now of our encounter with the other. T.S. Eliot was right: we have a long way to go, a long journey ahead before arriving at the present! Perhaps what we need is a new paradigm to discover the truth that dwells in every moment, in the here and now of every encounter. [...] Oedipus and Laius overflow with *hybris* and argue over the right of way. Who has precedence? The king or the passer-by? The young or the old man? This is their underlying mistake. You cannot be interested in the quest for truth and then battle over precedence. When travelling down the road of truth, right of way must always be given to others. Only by giving way and slowing down, showing respect for others, do we realise that truth is not an object to be pillaged or taken possession of, but something which should be awaited ("[it does] not need obstetric forceps," recites Whitman)[6] and searched for together, because truth belongs to everybody and to everybody it reveals itself—in reality just as it presents itself, in a rose just as it appears, in the face of the other, showing its footsteps and direction.
> [...]
> We set off, together with Oedipus and Laius, in search of truth and now we find ourselves in the crossroads of relationships. We have discovered that truth and relationships are intimately connected.[7] What is more, we have learnt that those who believe they possess truth can turn, as history teaches us, into murderers. The force of truth can be destructive if it is unleashed beyond the confines of relationships. And that is why the crossroads of truth brings us back to the crossroads of relationships.
>
> (Salonia 2005, pp. 31–35, my translation)

A reality-truth that does not encompass the relationship easily becomes fundamentalism. Fundamentalism is a closure that brings to the desire to eliminate not only the different other, but also the difference in the other. Madness, fundamentalism, and populism are all distortions, if not the outright annihilation, of reality. In the contemporary world, they are all signs of the lack of a third element in relationships and in society. In this book, we will increasingly see how otherness is only such if there exists a third element. If not, it becomes an unbridgeable gap or engulfment.

> In the ancient world, Greece included, interpersonal relationships were therefore always mediated by an Absolute, by a Third that avoided direct contact between people, symbolized by the community and its representatives. The community is seen as a single organism, a supreme good to which all the parts are pre-ordained.
>
> (Bruni 2012, p. 8)

In his book, Bruni suggests that the market is presently the third element interposed among humans, defining and regulating their relationships. Thus, in a forever partial, forever changing list, we can add the market and the community as third elements in interactions—without forgetting direction, meaning, ground, the relationship itself, and absolute otherness, which encompasses us and goes beyond us. Many possible ways of expressing, facing, and anchoring otherness alternate and overlap in different historical periods and different social and cultural contexts, shaping the contexts themselves in turn.

Today, in fragmented societies (Salonia 1999, 2000; Gecele & Francesetti 2007), in a fluctuating reality, more than ever before there is a need for a third element, a need to clarify it, to seek it, to not take it for granted. Since the early days of psychoanalysis, we have moved from a hierarchical society, in which triality was imposed through social rules—a ground of restrictions, roles, and social orders was present in every relationship and transaction—and internalized in a super-ego, to a triality to be defined in every single relationship, for which it is harder to construct and maintain.

> The problem that nagged Freud—how to foster the reality principle through education—is contextual to a symbiotic society. In a narcissistic society, a more radical question emerges: Who makes the rules? Up to what point must reality be respected? No reality should be experienced as preordained and unmodifiable—where does it say that reality cannot be modified? Who decided as much? In "narcissistic" society, guilt is about "not being oneself," about betraying oneself, and thus the face of the other, perceived as the bearer of rules and demands of affiliation, as an obstacle hindering one's self-fulfilment, slowly steps aside.
>
> (Salonia 2000, p. 104, my translation)

Let's broaden our sights

As we go deeper into our exploration of otherness, let's remember again how every thought, every perspective, every world view is situated within a specific historical, cultural, and experiential pathway. The reference to triality itself points to a possible derivation from a Jewish-Christian cultural ground.

Without backtracking on the arguments presented here on the importance of a third element in relationships, we should open the door to the hypothesis that the idea of the third element echoes the concept of Trinitarian perfection. The myth of fulfilment, which duality avoids, could therefore crop up again through triality. Stressing this cultural ground serves to avoid the risk of proposing yet again the utopia of a perfection within our grasp. The concept of triality that we are exploring here is a sign of multiplicity, possibility, absence, and the ineliminable limit of the human condition.

On the other hand, the polarity of dualism is not necessarily in itself negative. The risk lies in its fixation, rigidity, and sterile reflections. The East teaches us, through the Tao, how oppositions are continuously formed and resolved, in an incessant flow of life-in-process that also determines an intermediate point, a moment of surpassing, a sort of third polarity. Yin, Yang, and the Median Void (Cheng 2000) are the three possible condensations of the Breath of life, its three coexistent alternatives.

> [...] true beauty—beauty that occurs and is revealed, that just suddenly appears to touch the soul of the one who perceives it—results from the encounter between two beings or between the human spirit and the living universe. And the work of beauty, always arising from a "between," is a third thing that, springing from the interaction of the two, allows the two to surpass themselves. If there is transcendence, it lies in this surpassing.
> (Cheng 2009, p. 105)

Face-to-face with the foreigner

In making this journey towards the foreigner and considering the challenges of relationships in a plurality of cultures and worlds, we increasingly come to realise that what we are finding are also new insights into othernesses much closer to us, keys unlocking landscapes we thought we already knew. Focusing on more macroscopic differences can help us explore the prejudices and foreknowledge that conditions our daily life experience.

Even on the social and political plane, taking into account the presence of foreign immigrants when thinking, taking a stance, and acting raises issues that concern and touch us all in relation to the laws, practices, and customs of civil life and the accessibility of institutions and public services. We know all too well through daily experience how public services are often constructed in a self-referential way, and not in response to or through engagement with the needs of community members. By upsetting the equilibrium, immigrants open the loopholes in those practices, laying bare their limits and the need for their renewal.

Our being fully present in encounter implies, when we find ourselves face-to-face with a 'foreigner,' being aware of elements that we often leave in the ground—beliefs, habits, communication codes determined by our multiple social and cultural affiliations. We should not forget that the prejudices, expectations, and capabilities for deciphering differences circulating in the field include not only our own, but those of the people we are encountering. We are, and we are seen as, representatives of one or more social and cultural contexts. Even attribution mechanisms, as described by interpersonal communication theories, take on specific meanings within the framework of intercultural communication.

> An "attribution" error arises, according to Jones and Nisbett,[8] from the fact that a pervasive tendency is found in the perception of individual behaviour, for which every agent is inclined to attribute the fundamental causes of their own negative or inadequate actions to situational requirements, whereas an observer, in interpreting the behaviour, is inclined to consider dispositional qualities possessed by the agent as predominant. Explanations for this divergent tendency between the agent and observer should be sought, to begin with, in the fact that the agent has a wider and more differentiated knowledge of the circumstances, history, motivations, and experiences of their action. [...] For the observer, the behaviour stands out as "figure" against the "ground" constituted by the situation; whereas for the agent, the "figure" is constituted by situational cues, or factors that lead to the behaviour.
> (Franta & Salonia 1990, pp. 27–28, my translation)

In intercultural communication and relationships, often it is the 'other' who defines the behaviours, emotions, beliefs, and mindsets of the interlocutor as belonging to a cultural context and as coming from it. Foreigners—especially when an immigrant and so the object of a multiple attribution mechanism—thus remain caught in a hall of mirrors where they are continuously attributed the 'other' affiliation, such as being considered European in North Africa and North African in Europe, for instance. Personal traits and qualities thus become blurred and unclear.

It is easy, from the outside, to lump together the ways of thinking, speaking, and acting shared by groups of people from the same geographical, social, and cultural background. As therapists and educators, and also as politicians and citizens, the risk is that of considering them as such pathological, as different to a norm and hence in need of correction; or, on the contrary, as something completely and totally other to us and so not to be questioned or touched a priori. To lower these risks, we need to adapt to the intercultural sphere the qualities inherent in every contact process, in the continuous intersecting of the novel and the known. On the one hand, when face-to-face with a foreigner, we cannot go without a map, a ground of knowledge and experience, a foreknowledge that stands out in a clear and marked way. On the other hand, fluidness and openness are especially important, almost as though we should forget that same foreknowledge, as useful and inevitable as it is.

"You've never been there, I suppose."

"Where?"

Why was he being so bloody aggressive about it?

"You know where. Bombay, Delhi, Madras, Bangalore, Hyderabad, Trivundum, Goa, the Punjab. You've never had that dust in your nostrils?"

"Never in my nostrils, no."

"You must go," he said, as if nobody had ever been there but him.

"I will, OK?"

"Yes, take a rucksack and see India, if it's the last thing you do in your life."

"Right, Mr Shadwell."

He lived in his own mind, he really did. He shook his head then and did a series of short barks in his throat. This was him laughing, I was certain. "Ha, ha, ha, ha, ha!" he went. He said, "What a breed of people two hundred years of imperialism has given birth to. If the pioneers from the East India Company could see you. What puzzlement there'd be. Everyone looks at you, I'm sure, and thinks: an Indian boy, how exotic, how interesting, what stories of aunties and elephants we'll hear now from him. And you're from Orpington."

"Yeah."

"Oh God, what a strange world. The immigrant is the Everyman of the twentieth century. Yes?"

(Kureishi 2009, p. 141)

Notes

1 Lévinas E. (1981). *Otherwise than Being or Beyond Essence*. Translated by Alphonso Lingis. Dordrecht: Kluwer Academic Publishers.
2 Bateson G. (1972). *Steps to an Ecology of Mind*. Northvale, NJ: Jason Aronson Inc.
3 Lévinas E. (1981). *Otherwise than Being or Beyond Essence*. English translation by Alphonso Lingis. Dordrecht-Boston-London: Kluwer Academic Publishers.
4 An overview of the two positions in the Lévinas-Buber debate can be found in Mancini R. (1991). *La comunicazione come ecumene. Il significato antropologico e teologico dell'etica comunicativa*. Brescia: Queriniana. Buber M. (1970). *I and Thou*. Translated by Walter Kaufmann. New York: Charles Scribner's Sons.
5 A most pregnant example of this narrative style is the novel *The White Castle*. Translated by Victoria Holbrook (New York: George Braziller, 1990).

6 "All truths wait in all things, [...] They do not need the obstetric forceps of the surgeon ..." Walt Whitman, Song of Myself, 30. (in *Leaves of Grass*).
7 Salonia G. *Verità e relazioni. Tra fondamentalismo e relativismo*. Forthcoming.
8 Jones E.E., Nisbett R.E. (1972). The Actor and the Observer: Divergent Perceptions of Causes of Behavior. In E.E. Jones et al. *Attribution: Perceiving the Causes of Behavior*. Morristown, NY: General Learning Press, pp. 79–94 (80).

References

Ardener S.G. (1978). *The Nature of Women in Society*. London: Taylor & Francis.

Bruni L. (2012) *The Wound and The Blessing. Economics, Relationships, and Happiness*. Translated by N. Michael Brennan. New York: New City Press. Originally published as *La ferita dell'altro. Economia e relazioni umane*. Trento: Il Margine., 2007

Cavarero A. (2007). *Il femminile negato. La radice greca della violenza occidentale*. Villa Verucchio (RN): Pazzini Editore.

Cheng F. (2000). *The River Below*. Translated by Julia Shirek Smith. New York: Welcome Rain.

Cheng F. (2004). *Green Mountain, White Cloud. A Novel of Love in the Ming Dynasty*. Translated from the French by Timothy Bent. New York: St. Martin's Press.

Cheng F. (2009). *The Way of Beauty. Five Meditations for Spiritual Transformation*. Translated by Jody Gladding. Rochester, Vermont: Inner Traditions.

Franta H., Salonia G. (1990). *Comunicazione interpersonale*. Rome: LAS-Libreria Ateneo Salesiano.

Gecele M., Francesetti G. (2007) "The Polis as the Ground and Horizon of Therapy." In G. Francesetti (ed.), *Panic Attacks and Postmodernity. Gestalt Therapy Between Clinical and Social Perspectives*. Milan: FrancoAngeli, pp. 170–209. Originally published as "La polis come 'ground' e orizzonte della terapia. In G. Francesetti (ed.) *Attacchi di panico e postmodernità, la psicoterapia della Gestalt fra clinica e società*. Milan: FrancoAngeli, 2005.

Gilligan C. (1982). *In a Different Voice. Psychological Theory and Women's Development*. Cambridge (MA): Harvard University Press.

Gilligan C. (2003). *The Birth of Pleasure. A New Map of Love*. New York: Knopf Doubleday.

Kureishi H. (2009), *The Buddha of Suburbia*. London: Faber and Faber.

Lévinas E. (1987). *Collected Philosophical Papers*. Translated by Alphonso Lingis. Dordrecht: Martinus Nijhoff Publishers.

Lévinas E. (1999). *Alterity and Transcendence*. Translated by Michael B. Smith. London: The Athlone Press. Translated in Italian as *Alterità e trascendenza*. Genoa: Il melangolo, 2006.

Maher V. (1992). *Il latte materno. I condizionamenti culturali di un comportamento*. Turin: Rosenberg & Sellier.

Mead M. (1967). *Male and Female: A Study of the Sexes in a Changing World*. New York: William Morrow.

Pamuk O. (2006). *Istanbul. Memories and the City*. Translated by Maureen Freely. New York: Vintage Books. Translated in Italian as *Istanbul*. Turin: Einaudi, 2006.

Rubin G. (2004). "The Traffic in Women." In J. Rivkin, M. Ryan (ed.) *Literary Theory: An Anthology*. Blackwell, Malden, MA, 770–794.

Salonia G. (1999). "Dialogare nel tempo della frammentazione." In F. Rametta, M. Naro (ed.) *Impense Adlaboravit*. Palermo: Facoltà Teologica di Sicilia.

Salonia G. (2000). "La criminalità giovanile tra vecchie e nuove regole. Verso l'integrazione dello straniero nella polis." *Quaderni di Gestalt XX*, 30/31, 100–108.

Salonia G. (2005). "Il lungo viaggio di Edipo dalla legge del padre alla verità della relazione." In P. Argentino (ed.) *Tragedie greche e psicopatologia*. Siracusa: Medicalink Publishers.

Salonia G. (2007). *Odòs*. Bologna: EDB.

Salonia G. (2004a). "Femminile e maschile: vicende e significati di un'irriducibile diversità." In R.G. Romano (ed.) *Ciclo di vita e dinamiche educative nella società postmoderna*. Milan: FrancoAngeli.

Salonia G. (2004b). *Sulla felicità e dintorni. Tra corpo, tempo e parola*. Ragusa: ARGO Edizioni.

Žižek S. (2002). *Welcome to the Desert of the Real*. London/New York: Verso.

4 Invisible Grounds

The human drive to encounter the other aims ceaselessly to construct common grounds of experience and meaning, which make communication and contact possible. Even the course this book takes aims to construct grounds and support therapists, educators, workers, and all people in dwelling in them and assimilating them. The concept of ground, in its polarity with the concept of figure, is central in Gestalt theory, implying a never-ending process or movement between what stands out at the forefront and what feeds into and nourishes it. Can we find any synonyms for it? Partial synonyms might be context, scenario, field, frame, or hidden polarity, for instance.

Travelling through grounds

The ground encompasses all that concerns us as human beings—all relationships, all events, everything that happens and has happened, the conquests, the connections, along with all that is unfinished and what has not emerged. But the awareness of our being part of broader processes can only be expanded in a gradual way, through a striving towards otherness and the unknown that never completely loses its impetus. Expanding awareness comes through the ability to stay with the indefinite and the unsaid, to give time and support for the assimilation of any sort of experience, but also to dwell in the aurora of any encounter or event, sensing its potentialities and its risks when nothing has happened yet and the figure has still to form. To come face-to-face with otherness, it is important to remain aware that we can only ever catch a glimpse of the mystery of the other, without ever grasping it. The challenge lies in dwelling in dense and shifting scenarios, while keeping up roles, loyalties, and affiliations, or adjusting them gradually. The connection with the ground is also memory, both individual and collective, helping us to break free of rigid patterns and prejudices, as well as from fundamentalism. But it is a process that requires support, on the relational, social, and political planes.

> Fundamentalism is a stage that serves to push us to seek the other and/or the community, even though, in this process, feelings of fear are present

in relation to a world perceived as complex and fragmented, tricky and incomprehensible. [...] If fundamentalism is a necessary stage in the relational development of the person, and if the temptation to stop at this stage, in the culture of today, has become predominant, the especially urgent educational task thus becomes that of inventing pathways/itineraries (*odopoietikòs* was the name/task of the philosopher in ancient Greece) that enable fundamentalism, in the experience of every person and every group, not to be denied or overcome, but to be gone through. [...] When listened to at depth, our/others' (the distinction no longer appears significant) fundamentalism puts us in touch with our deepest fears, with our disorientation and disintegration anxieties, archaic anxieties that remind us of pre-verbal experiences of helplessness, of total dependency, and of the need for containment—the feeling of chaos, of being without direction in the world and in life, the anxiety of "foundations that shake," the dread of "being-thrown-into-the-world," to use Heidegger's words.

(Salonia 2007, pp. 150ff., my translation)

The 'in-between'

The possibility of achieving full and nourishing contact is given by drawing ceaselessly on the changing and complex grounds that constitute the 'in-between' (Francesetti & Gecele 2009). On the other hand, when time stops for an instant and is accomplished in contact, in an authentic presence that makes contents fade away and every other parameter disappear, the grounds are enriched in turn, changing the present moment and history. What happens in that instant between two people, or between groups of people, echoes in and constructs the world.

> Living together in the world essentially means there exists a world of things between those who share it, like a table situated between the people sitting around it. Like every in-between, the world connects and separates people at one and the same time. The public sphere, as a shared world, unites us, and yet it stops us from falling over each other, so to speak. What makes mass society so hard to bear is not, or at least not primarily, the number of people that make it up, but the fact that the world in between them has lost its power to unite them, to connect them and separate them.
>
> (Riva 1999, p. 39, my translation)

Hannah Arendt (1968, 1998) stresses the importance of the space constructed by and between people and made real by the shared awareness of moving within it. The *polis* is the place of the many, the dialectical space of exchange and reciprocal limitation, as opposed to the *oikos*, the home, the place of the few and of intimacy. The space 'in-between' is at once the place and time in which interaction, assimilation, and change happen, and the ground from which every figure emerges and to which every figure returns, where it dissolves but remains in memory. The in-between encompasses the world; it presupposes it and recreates it.

Otherness as ground

Fostering in others and oneself the capacity to listen and accept difference, to appreciate the mystery and truth of the other (Salonia 2007), constructs a fertile groundwork on which to stand. It is the premise that can pave the way to moments of true contact, of true presence. Vice versa, when the expectation in a relationship is of total and resolute encounter, the risk is that of a prevailing bitterness over what is lacking, over the failed promise of mutual understanding.

Knowing that irreducible otherness exists is part of the ground of every authentic relational experience. Without an awareness of the ground, the third entity is lacking in relationships and we risk remaining imprisoned in duality, in irresolvable contrapositions or in a confluence/engulfment that can even lead to shared psychosis.

> A dyad that excludes all external references leads towards death, because it decays into "folie à deux." A third entity is the reference point that prevents the flattening of the horizon for the dyad, continuously pushing it towards the experience of real encounter, which is always a "merging of horizons" (*Horizontverschmelzung*).
> (Salonia 2007, p. 153, my translation)

The presence and awareness of a third point of reference anchors and delimits the dual relationship, preventing us from seeing the other merely as the answer to our needs or, vice versa, as someone who is a threat to our well-being. In both these cases, specular as they are, the risk is that the interlocutor is not the bearer of a real and concrete presence. Seeking solely our own well-being or adapting totally to the needs and desires of others, building up frustration and resentment, are not real and fertile experiences of contact. The awareness of want, of need, of non-self-sufficiency are signs of relational maturity, connecting up with the horizon and very meaning of existence, to the vital ground in which the encounter and the relationship are situated. By inflicting a wound, marking out a boundary, calling us to take responsibility, the other gives meaning to our being in the world. Without the wound inflicted by otherness, the relationship loses all meaning, as does our narrative of ourselves, which is nourished by otherness. The attempt to make contact thus becomes compulsive, a barren attempt that can be repeated to infinity (Salonia 2004). It is relationships themselves that support the discovery of the very otherness that is the premise of relationships. Moreover, it is important not to seek the figure of contact too prematurely in relationships. When differences in personal stories, pathways, and horizons are too great, it takes lengthy listening and patient waiting before the presumption of encounter can be entertained.

> Relationships and contact need to be seen within the Gestalt framework of figure/ground for their connections and their ineliminable cross-references to be understood. From the ground/relationship emerges the figure/contact. The quality of the figure/contact is an expression of the ground/relationship and affects it.
>
> (Salonia 2001, p. 69, my translation)

The philosophical issues of ethics and responsibility—so vivid in the twentieth century—indissolubly interconnect with the relational issues addressed in psychotherapy. The contraposition of morality and law, of the needs and interests of the individual and those of the collective—depicted so well in Greek tragedy—have retreated into the background today, replaced by the importance and the centrality of the existence of the other, the essential and non-accidental premise for every individual existence.

The figure/ground dynamic: The ground comes to the fore

> The end of bipolarity expresses and provokes, at the social level, the disintegration of bonds at every level. It is the definitive death of "fathers," the symbolic passing of "objective" points of reference. The absence of strong and hierarchical affiliations is experienced, however, in a contradictory way. At first [...] there is a feeling of euphoria at having definitively broken free of all control, the inevitable interpretation of every affiliation. After that, however, experiences of disorientation and disintegration take over. Nobody takes care of anybody; if nobody has the power of control, nobody can give confirmation, if nobody can lay down prohibitions, there is no "authority figure" against which to fight, to test one's strength and shape one's identity. [...] Social disintegration can provoke the disorientation of the subject, who always needs to come face-to-face with another in order to construct and define themselves. One of the riskiest outcomes of disintegration is when it takes the form of the internal fragmentation of the subject's meanings, which are no longer drawn together into unity and utterability, due to the lack of a relationship that activates processes for deciphering and sharing experiences.
>
> (Salonia 1999, pp. 574–575, my translation)

When parts of the ground—relational, historical, social parts—are not integrated through awareness and contact, they remain unbridled and unpredictable, ready to become loose cannon at any moment, striking individuals and the community by surprise. Another consequence of not nourishing and not being nourished by the ground is that the potentialities, capabilities, and energy available for constructing figures—relationships, life plans, artistic creations, actions—are reduced. Resources slip away from us, in terms of information, possibilities for encounter, dialogue, and growth.

We are increasingly inclined to interpret the problematic issues we encounter and the challenges engaging us as concerning the ground more than the figure. Even the psychopathological suffering we encounter is an expression of our social and cultural context and calls for the priority to be focused on the construction of the ground, so as both to reconstruct the meaning of the suffering and to activate therapeutic interventions (Spagnuolo Lobb 2001a, 2007a; Gecele & Francesetti 2007; Francesetti & Gecele 2009; Gecele 2014, 2019).

> Personality disorders are a stronger call to society and to field than an isolated neurotic symptom is or was. They are a way of seeing, an imitation, an amplification, sometimes even a way to solve social issues. They are the ethnic disorder of our time (Devereux 1980; Gecele 2014). In these experiences, the social field is particularly strong in shaping themes, problems, solutions, and creative adaptations. [...] Considering the background and the context gives us support and keys to interpretation, it gives us more tools to work with "personality disorders."
>
> (Gecele 2019, p. 203)

Complexity, simplification, and emptiness: Forms of suffering

We live in a complex world. As much as we try to broaden our awareness, too many stimuli bombard us at every instant. Figures do not have the time they need to emerge and take shape, resulting in "a false integration of [...] experience" (Perls et al. 1994, p. 108). Creative adjustment today is primarily a matter of selection. It is about not losing the sense of direction that feeling needs and listening to the body gives. It is about maintaining the drive of relational intentionality, the ability to discern and orient oneself, the support of pathways, roles, and belonging. All this to give order to the disorder of chaos, to the complexity of the environment. A surplus of stimuli can lower the capacity/possibility of being present in relationships and the experience of emotions. Thus everything that can give the necessary support for distinguishing and deciphering those stimuli becomes fundamental for constructing a web of sense, meaning, and connection.

At the same time, especially in the arts—literature, cinema, music—and the human sciences, dwelling in the present with awareness also means complexifying. These two, apparently opposite directions are connected. If stimuli are not selected and not distinguished, there can be no possibility of choice. The risk is of over-simplifying, of making random choices, eliminating not difficulty, but complexity. That is also why prematurely seeking out a figure, clear outlines for a phenomenon, or an unequivocal position to take, can today be confusing and alienating. In situations of disorientation, confusion, and a lack of awareness, the search for apparent clarity can become a short-cut, a way of trimming back the complexity without working through it. In our day and age, it is not very instructive to speak of encounter and contact with otherness as a ready experience that is easy to achieve, an attainable goal within everybody's reach at any time, because in suggesting that it is, we may create the illusion of a facile well-being, where differences can be wiped out like magic. The priority instead is to learn to listen to diversity.

Although it is true that full encounter and contact—a moment of indefinite duration—is important, the concept of 'fullness' can be misleading. To use a provocation, it can be compared to the effect of a drug. Psychotropic substances create an artificial state of excitement and activation or, alternatively, of relaxation. What they do above all, however, is transiently fill a void. Taking drugs can conjure the illusion of being open and present with all the senses and with awareness. But it is just a mirage, the glimpse—almost the touch—of a possibility which instead is being pushed away. The figure is ephemeral, disconnected from the flow of time and from the constitution of meaning. It does not come from the ground and it does not return to it. The illusion of being open to encounter amounts to an attempt to reach it via a short-cut, without bringing along the baggage of one's history and wounds and depriving the figure of the complexity that lies in the ground. If contact is gone through in this way, assimilating the experience becomes very difficult, if not impossible. Just as change, the true grasping of novelty, becomes impossible. The illusion of a total closeness that is easy to attain and that fulfils our every need shows another side of the fear of the other, another face of fundamentalism. Extreme forms of the illusion determine manifestations of relational suffering that can go as far as psychopathology.

> The disturbances that accompany the difficulty of self-definition can take forms so subtle and unpronounced that they are never directly observed clinically. Nonetheless, they reduce the individual's capacity to take initiatives, plan, act in solidarity, and open out to a common social dimension.[1] "It becomes very difficult to realize oneself when one is overcome with thousands of possible networks of belonging and an infinite number of possibilities that are often unattainable—when one is faced with the relativization of every norm."[2] A number of observers have indeed noted an increasingly widespread ill-being, which is indefinite, vague, sometimes depressive, sometimes anxious, and difficult to pin down in terms of clear psychopathological categories or precise sociopathological manifestations.[3] Sociopathological behaviors can, in part, be understood as an outward expression of the individual's difficulty in constructing his or her personal identity—a process that always occurs through the recognition of the Other in a continuous and significant relationship. Violence

today is often accompanied by an experience of existential emptiness, a nonperception of limits, and a blindness towards the needs, pain, and even existence of the Other-as-subject. This "relational immaturity" manifests itself in violence at the very moments when the control and the norms of society become uncertain and undefined, with the result that violence can be avoided only through a capacity to recognize the Other's dignity, otherness, and personality. Where personal vulnerability encounters a collective experience of disorientation, psychopathic or sociopathic behaviors can easily result. This is due to the lack of sufficient relational support (from the family or community) to contain the personal disturbance and to orient the individual through ties of belonging.

To give another example, substance abuse has also been profoundly altered by our contemporary context. It no longer represents an attempt to differentiate oneself by rebelling against a social norm but rather stems from an inability to live through meaningful experiences. This leads to an internal vacuum[4] and a relational desert, which often fails to inspire the sorrow that would afford meaning to the experience. Rather, meaningful experience is passed through with an anaesthetized indifference in which substance abuse at least offers an opportunity to "feel" something.

(Gecele & Francesetti 2007, pp. 186–187)

The 'liquidity' of grounds

Our societies—societies Bauman describes as 'liquid'[5]—tend to deprive themselves of their own grounds, of the affiliations, othernesses, and shared world that we are all called to construct. In both public life and in intimate relationships, constructing a shared reality is far from easy, and its lack makes it harder for a figure to stand out clearly, remaining hazy and unstable instead. This raises the bar for perceiving every experience, with the risk that only strong emotions are felt. Even the bar for seeing the other is high. Acts of self-harm and anti-social behaviour are articulations of the great effort being made to shut out the feeling of devastating solitude, of the search for a perception of the other in the form of rules, limits, and intervention.

> In the fragmentation stage, the level of confusion rises dramatically. Pluricentricity hinders the formation of the meaning of one's own integrity and unity, determining a disintegration and confusion of identity ("Beyond the subject"), a "zapping personality" incapable of constituting itself as subject, as a partner in an interaction. Rules are not perceived because they seem to be empty vessels. One is not against, but outside of this logic. The question that comes with destructive potential is thus, what is real and what is not? It is the fragmentation and confusion of every identity without bounds, because if, on the one hand, bounds limit identity, on the

other, they determine it. Criminal actions are on the rise which appear to be an unwitting and pressing call for "containment." Certain youths repeat at-risk behaviours harming themselves or others as though they were seeking a place (often prison) in which to contain their feelings of boundless and fragmented divinity. It would appear significant that—as the statistics tell us—offences against the person are on the rise, as though there were a desperate desire to measure oneself against the other in "mortal" violence, which for a moment lets you open your eyes and realize there is a presence. [...] Subjectivity and disintegration are the interpretative premises we use for analysing the criminal phenomena of today.

(Salonia 2000, p. 104, my translation)

Globalization has led certain affiliations to come apart, throwing into the ground, more so than in the past, the entire world. Here we are not talking about a ground that is constructed and perceived through heightening awareness, but a ground of unfinished possibilities and changes, of excess stimuli, and a lack of pauses. Only a small part of that world, made up primarily of bits of information, pictures, and sketchy experiences, can be explored and assimilated within a significant relationship. Indeed, the relational support needed to expand awareness is often lacking. Everything seems to be present and within reach, but it is so hard to grasp and take hold of, engendering disorientation, confusion, renunciation, and a sense of not knowing how to give shape to chaos. This paves the way to the risk of taking simplified routes, of believing in any possible solution whatsoever, without checking its validity, in an effort to sort things out and find a 'safe' place in which to stay. These routes that lead to strict affiliations and distorted identifications can be countered, if not avoided, by supporting—on various planes, including the institutional and educational levels—authentic encounters and relationships. This brings us back to the importance of people who work 'on the margins.' Alongside artists and therapists, they also include educators and trainers, but potentially also policy-makers, professionals, tradespeople, and community members. The idea again put forth here is that creative adjustment, in today's world, is increasingly less about the figures that take shape and increasingly more about the capacity to dwell in grounds, to bear the anxiety that can come when not seeking out in haste solutions, figures, and forms that are pre-determined and defined. A form/figure determined in haste, because anxiety and uncertainty are felt to be too great to bear, is often constructed on a void. Rigidity, such as in the form of relativism, and shapelessness, such as when definitions are too clear-cut, emerge from a lack in the ground.

Time and space in emigration

People who emigrate often do so for contingent and concrete reasons, be they economic, social, cultural, religious, or political, and hence with a desire to change their status and condition. Or they might do so because they feel constrained and limited within their customary world, because they have, or feel they have, no prospects and opportunities. Even if we are not referring here to refugees, to the experience of fleeing from war, famine, and natural disasters, in migratory processes the need for support is especially strong. The country a migrant imagines and expects to find never matches the one they ultimately find themselves in. That is often the case in terms of objective parameters and elements, but it is definitively always true in terms of the feeling of belonging, ties and relationships, and the sense of connection with the environment. The decision to leave one's home and emigrate transforms the flow of time, just as much as it modifies space. And as we know, time and relationships are connected.

> Time defines our identity and our relationships as it determines their inevitable changes and reveals their deeper structures. In an increasingly clearer way, the connection between time and relationships proves to be vital. It is no coincidence that Levinas saw in time and otherness the original coordinates of every subjectivity. [...] If, on the one hand, we receive the notion of time from an affective relationship, on the other, we learn what a relationship is from time.
>
> (Salonia 2004, pp. 144–145, my translation)

The decision to emigrate determines a change in the way relationships and affiliations are lived, which is why it modifies time. Before setting off, if the migration plans are shared and have a collective dimension, or if they have strong support and encouragement, time becomes compressed and is annihilated, in much the same way as happens in manic episodes of mood disorders. When the new country is reached, however—and especially when support is lacking to cope with the overwhelming novelty encountered and correlated loss of habits, affects, language, social and relational skills, flavours, smells, and codes—the risk is that time dilates and space becomes disconnected from the body, in a comparable way to what happens in depressive experience. These passages can be found in many accounts of migration experiences, indicating a rift in the coexistence of meaning and experience. "Thus, we must not say that our body is in space, nor for that matter in time. It inhabits space and time" (Merleau-Ponty 2012, p. 140). People who emigrate are likely to feel a lack of basic support, where such support encompasses the way the body inhabits the world. That lack undermines the sense of legitimacy in occupying a place in the world, in being a part of it—a sense given by the capacity to interact, deliberately and effectively, with the environment. Along with the things they perhaps wanted to change, migrants also lose some of the certainties that are part of the bodily, verbal, and relational ground taken for granted, and which enable them to give continuity to experience and deal with novelty. Roles and memories can lose meaning in a context of migration and, transiently at least, disintegrate or freeze. The sense of continuity in shaping and conceiving one's life can even breakdown completely.

Let's draw again on Merleau-Ponty's words, this time to explore the support afforded by continuity in experience and by a shared history.

> When I chat with a close friend, each of his words and each of mine contains, beyond what they signify for everyone else, a multitude of references to the principal dimensions of his personality and of mine, without our needing to evoke our previous conversations. These acquired worlds, which give my experience its secondary sense, are themselves cut out of a primordial world that grounds the primary sense of my experience. Similarly, there is a "world of thoughts," a sedimentation of our mental operations, which allows us to count on our acquired concepts and judgments, just as we count upon the things that are there and that are given as a whole, without our having to repeat their synthesis at each moment. This is how for us there can be a sort of mental panorama with its accentuated regions and its confused regions, a physiognomy of questions, and intellectual situations such as research, discovery, and certainty. But this word "sedimentation" should not trick us: this contracted knowledge is not an inert mass at the foundation of our consciousness. [...] Likewise, my acquired thoughts are not an absolute acquisition; they feed off my present thought at each moment; they offer me a sense, but this is a sense that I reflect back to them.
>
> (Merleau-Ponty 2012, pp. 131–132)

One's country of origin provides a shared linguistic and communicative framework that also allows us to express and make use of our knowledge and know-how to the full. For knowledge and know-how, just like behaviours, only make sense in a given setting, where they are appreciated and used best. Such knowledge and know-how are forged by an emergent drive within the emotional, relational, and material climate found in that determinate context.

Habits

It must be stressed how habits are similarly relational and tied to the setting. When dwelling in an experience comes spontaneously, established habits continue to redefine themselves and be modified. On the contrary, in situations of distress, as in certain phases of the migration process, habits not tied to the flow of the experience of the self can become constituted and reinforced. There can be a fixation with old habits that lose their meaning and purpose in the new context, depleting the resources available for creative adjustments to be made to the new setting; or new habits might be formed that, in a dysfunctional way, become a sort of obsessive ritual, a way of releasing anxiety and giving shape and meaning to the field. Other possibilities are that elements of the new setting—lifestyles and relational styles—are uncritically absorbed and swallowed up whole, or that old habits disintegrate, leaving a vacuum filled by chaos. Thus, instead of new creative adjustments, we find confusion and fragmentation, and a resulting difficulty in going through and situating experiences. On the other hand, positive connections, satisfying and reassuring experiences, and hence adequate support can promote, in a new context, the assimilation of habits uncritically introjected in the past, in the places of one's birth and original belonging.

> In Goodman's terms, the assimilated habit, fruit of the effective conquest of the experience and thus a part of the organism, is no longer contacted, but is always available to consciousness. The case is different with a habit that consolidates in an unconscious way, where the person is not able to realize it. It signals none other than an interruption in the flow of experience; when contact fails, what is learnt is just a way, for sure the best possible way, of adapting to a difficult field, an attempt to keep the dangers of the emergency under control, which soon becomes fixed in an unchangeable pattern that goes against any confident abandonment to the flow of things, because it aims solely to avoid the risk of anxiety returning.
> (Sichera 2001, p. 24, my translation)

When we step into a new context, greater or lesser parts of the ground (by which I mean new habits, affects, language, relational and social skills, flavours, smells, and codes) require reconstruction. An emptiness, a lack of direction, a tendency to feel helpless in trying to reach the other can all be perceived in the relational field in the degree of presence. Emptiness and helplessness call for greater drive, energy, and willpower for encounter to be possible. If the present experience lacks a ground on which to take shape— a ground made up of knowledge, habits, and environmental support—then everything is novel. Such novelty, however, can be perilous and threatening; it can lead to frustration, isolation, and unconnectedness, or the experience of feeling invaded by an incomprehensible environment. All this tends to give shape to forms of experience that in some way offer protection from relational distress. Phenomena can arise that recall depressive experiences, or even show paranoic or obsessive aspects,[6] where the latter are characterized by the impossibility of trusting and relying on the basic, given certainties underpinning everyday life and relationships.

Another risk is that, to avoid emptiness, a migrant may keep a strong, unconscious, and uncritical bond with a rigidly fixed ground which does not belong to the present context but to crystallized fragments of the past, and thus reduces or prevents presence in present relational fields.

Both when the ground dissolves and when it becomes fixed, the figure may crystallize or, in more extreme situations, it may itself become fragmented. The lack of confidence in the possibility of undergoing new experiences of contact by going beyond one's present certainties does not permit the mobility needed for the self to express itself and the figure/ground dynamic to flow.

The culture experienced by the migrant as the 'mother' culture is often not a dynamic process, but a frozen memory, something fixed that does not match up with the continuous construction and transformation of reality. That rigid figure/ground incorporates and is fuelled by the point of view of the host society when it is all-encompassing or, at the other extreme, rejecting, when the 'other' is experienced as an "invader" with the power apparently to wipe out all that we feel to be the most intimate part of us, the foundations of our narrative. Prejudice, as an attitude that defines and distances, protects against the invasion.

Even when the figure/ground process becomes rigid in the field constituted by the interaction between the migrant and the host society, what we are dealing with is still a process of creative adjustment, and it is important to support its constructive aspects. Support is always the main counter-measure for the risks we have been describing—not to avoid suffering, but to prevent its fixation as absence, and hence as psychopathology (Francesetti 2016). So as to foster instead more vital and functional creative adjustments.

The ground in time: Memory and history

Memory—both individual and collective—is a ground that is in constant movement and construction. It is the groundwork on which we construct social connections, values, and affiliations. The individual and collective memory process requires great care, demanding constant attention and maintenance. Disorientation and disintegration anxieties can lead us to lock up and solidify, or alternatively to simplify and sweeten, a past that is often a place and source of pain, a past that can only be worked through at times with major relational support.

Even when we shift into the horizon of the past, we come up against the risk of fundamentalism. It is easy for us to lose our connection with history and with histories, leaving us unprepared to face the figures of today, which through that disconnection have become too novel, unexpected, and threatening.

> To remember is not to bring back before the gaze of consciousness a self-subsistent picture of the past, it is to plunge into the horizon of the past and gradually to unfold tightly packed perspectives until the experiences that it summarizes are as if lived anew in their own temporal place. To perceive is not to remember.
> (Merleau-Ponty 2012, p. 23)

The dimension of collective memory is especially complex, forming a terrain on which the distortions of individual memory intersect and combine with a multitude of other factors. The information of today and historical construction mutually influence, construct, and deconstruct each other, in a continuous, reciprocal conditioning.

> Various social and historical groups fighting for information strive to monopolize it. The means used towards this end vary between secret texts and codes (the secret languages of different age and social groups; religious, political and professional secrets, etc.) and the creation of misleading texts. Wherever instantaneous usage is in force, falsehood cannot arise. It grows on the same basis as information does and represents the reverse side of its social functioning.
>
> (Lotman 1976, p. 215)

Boundary figures and prophetic figures in the polis

Often it is people who live on the margins, at the boundaries of a social and cultural context, a geographical place, or a historical period that are most sensitive to the ground. Artists can be seen to live 'at the boundary' (Spagnuolo Lobb & Amendt-Lyon 2007). Perhaps therapists do too.[7]

If, in a society, awareness of the ground is found only in the few, if there is little sharing of history, memory, the implicit, the unsaid, and the unspeakable, then the burden on the individual becomes greater, it becomes 'prophetic.' In societies, just as in groups, many voices articulate the polyphony of the field. But what if the voices remain silent? If nobody embodies them? There probably is not enough support for them to take shape and express themselves, for them to be listened to, which determines a non-hearing, an inability to speak, a lack of true words.

Thus a heightening responsibility falls on those burdened by too many perceptions, words, actions, and gestures in search of an author. This prophet, voice not of the divine but of the field, risks being isolated, attacked, and misunderstood. Boundary figures are often prophetic, giving voice to otherness, to what is taking shape, to what tends to come from the ground to become figure. The stress here is on the importance for the therapist to live at the boundaries, to train and work on dwelling in grounds, so as to develop a unique sensibility.

Every era, culture, and society gives privilege to and highlights certain themes, leaving others in the shadows. They bring into focus relational approaches, ways of being in society, which stand out from the infinite possibilities of creating and regulating our being humans. Culture, in its plurality of acceptations, helps us find direction and make sense of experience, without having to start all over again from scratch every time, as though there were no history, or rather histories of humankind to give shape and order to individual life. The relational, institutional, and economic framework of the sociocultural context in which we live provides us with a clearly outlined map, albeit one in continuous transformation. That entails risks and limits that are different and specific to every model of society.

What is common to all human groups, however, is the presence of a gap between the map used and reality. If that gap exceeds a certain threshold, the risk is that of living in a construct of humanity and relationships that falls short of life itself, never managing to touch it. In our 'western' contexts, that risk is heightened all the more the means and tools for passing on information prevail over the content, speed over concentration, impressions over facts, and the importance of novelty over the cultivation of memory. In this way, figures—news and information, fashions and trends, but also values and forms of relationships—can be mystifying (Gecele & Francesetti 2007). Knowing how to dwell in the ground means not being dazzled by figures, especially when they are artifacts, when they are products of consumption or the fruit of thought that is not critical and not criticizable.

Disclosing the fiction as a support for approaching the other

Fiction can be considered a part of the shared social ground and framework. Every society constructs an order, a lifestyle, and values, determining affiliations and otherness. They define figures and ground, building a structure that is artificial but indispensable, a fiction, a script to follow.

Otherness is therefore already present in the awareness that social life is not a natural process but a construction, reminding us that there are an infinite number of other possible constructions. Social maturity thus lies in the possibility of seeing the fiction for what it is. The passage into adult life, marked by initiation rites, would appear to suggest just that.

> How often are we led to find (with pleasant surprise) that in many initiation rituals, usually so cruel and painful, the objective is not to forcefully introject into young people the group's values and beliefs, but to take them behind the scenes to see, in an entirely laic way, the mechanism of social "fiction" and power. "Us men are the true tambaran" (the monster that swallows children) is what is said to the initiates of a society of West New Britain.[8] That is, it is not a mystical and transcendent truth that is revealed; it is the fiction that is revealed and explained.[9]
>
> (Remotti 2006, pp. 52–53, my translation)

The more one's roots are criticized, relativized, accepted, and chosen, the more one can be open to other possibilities and be present and active in the melting pot in which social and cultural processes, exchanges, and hybridizations are forged. The process of assimilating 'us' is, at the same time, a path of transformation into all that from which we come and the acquisition of a critical—laic—view of it. Disconnection from the flow in which we are inserted instead fosters closure and rigid fixation. The widespread inability to reach a critical viewpoint on one's socio-cultural context is one of the causes of individual and social instability and of possible rigid fixations. Paradoxically, if a critical lucidness of one's context is lacking, it is impossible to arrive at the next step, one that cannot be taken for granted, which is consciously choosing to belong to it.

An aspect of the context in which we live is that it is so complex as to render it necessary—in an effort to orient ourselves—to continuously delegate to and place our trust in specialists in various sectors. This fosters a sort of progressive desensitization in the individual and in groups, because where the capability to see is fragmented, the harder it is to understand social mechanisms and develop a critical capacity. Dwelling in grounds, expanding awareness of the complexity of the field (Spagnuolo Lobb 2004), and supporting others—the community in which one lives—all reduces the social risks of mystification and manipulation. This connects closely with intercultural issues as they are, by definition, the origin and product of complexity. In addressing grounds and social fictions, the scant awareness of them therefore becomes a limit that is greatly conditioning. "Reality does not 'reside' in the organism-subject, nor in the environment-object, but rather in their unitary encounter and interaction, at the ever-mobile contact boundary that their mutual experience of each other produces" (Cavaleri 2003, p. 72, my translation).

From the human polis to spirituality

If we do not see the other, if we miss their story, provenance, construction, and vision of life, then we do not see a piece of the general ground. The figure that forms in contact is less vivid, less real and transformative if there is no awareness of having come from different paths; the implicit transcendence of relational intentionality loses direction and meaning. And the greater the differences are, as a premise for encounter, the more that risk is present. "Accepting diversity means not positing its understanding as a condition for trusting and caring for the other. Seeking to understand is necessary, but it is also necessary not to persist obstinately: The mystery of the other also needs to be respected" (Salonia 2007, p. 182, my translation).

Accepting the wound and limit imposed by the very existence of the other does not eliminate suffering, but it avoids the harm caused by refusing and denying the reality. Unfortunately, though, it often seems easier to take refuge in the presumption of self-sufficiency.

The mystery and unknowability of otherness is part of the ground of our being humans. They point to a beyond that we can never entirely conquer or understand. In the space-time in which we live, perhaps we should constantly remember, in every relationship, that we cannot understand each other and reach each other; that we are free not to understand each other, but at the same time we are free to keep trying. Derrida (1995)—moving within a phenomenological horizon—tells us that alterity is given precisely by the continuous impossibility of encounter, by a presence that is only a trace and absence. If total encounter were possible, true otherness could not exist.[10] In this understanding of it, God becomes the absolute singularity of the other, and the voice of alterity is the voice of God.[11]

When something or somebody, or a faith, which need not be religious, gives direction to life, pointing the way beyond, this gives support and meaning to everyday life. The process is circular, reciprocal, and co-present. At every moment, encounters and contacts nurture a human growth that is also spiritual and transcendent.

Notes

1 Crespi F. (2002). *Le identità distruttive e il problema della solidarietà* [Destructive Identities and the Problem of Solidarity]. International Seminar in Memory of Alberto Melucci: "Identità e movimenti sociali in una società planetaria". Milan, 11–12 October 2002.

2 Salonia G. (1999). "Dialogare nel tempo della frammentazione." In F. Armetta, M. Naro (eds.) *Impense adlaboravit*. Palermo: Facoltà Teologica di Sicilia, pp. 571–586. [Quote translated from the Italian by A. Spencer.]

3 This general ill-being can also manifest itself in more evident clinical disorders. Hence, the increase in identity disorder, personality disorders, and acute symptoms in general (Melucci 1996, Ehrenberg 1999, Pavan 2002).

The rise in the number of individuals suffering from panic attacks is another such example (Gerdes 1995). Panic attacks are most common in contexts characterized by interpersonal ties and social networks that are fragile, uncertain, and fragmentary (Pavan 2002), but which simultaneously afford the individual the possibility of attaining to the kind of awareness panic represents, the 'laceration' to which we referred earlier; in Gecele & Francesetti 2005.

4 Beaugrand S. (1999) "A propos d'une production sociale des borderlines." *Cahiers de Gestalt 6*.

5 Zygmunt Bauman wrote extensively on the topic. His works include *Liquid Times: Living in an Age of Uncertainty*, Cambridge: Polity, 2007, *Community. Seeking Safety in an Insecure World*, Cambridge: Polity, 2001, and *Liquid Love: On the Frailty of Human Bonds*, Cambridge: Polity, 2003.

6 The Gestalt therapy approach to psychopathology and diagnosis is relational and field-oriented. Great attention is placed on the context and suffering is never attributed to the individual, but is specifically situated in the 'between' of the relationship (Francesetti & Gecele 2009). The reference to terminology derived from psychopathology does not seek here to 'pathologize' the individual, but to contribute to describing the relational and social suffering felt widely, mutually, and contextually in migration experiences.

7 "The perception of reality, the experience we have of it as the reality of the field (field organization), can be ascribed, more than to the emerging need, 'to all that series of vivid relationships that take place at the boundary,' made up of struggle and concrete manipulation, of sentiments and communication." (Cavaleri 2001, p. 59)

8 Lattas A (1989). "Trickery and Sacrifice: Tambarans and Appropriation of Female Reproductive Powers in Male Initiation Ceremonies in West New Britain." *Man* XXIV, pp. 451–69.

9 Remotti F. (2000). *Prima lezione di antropologia*. Bari: Laterza, pp. 100–109.

10 "If signifying were equivalent to indicating, a face would be insignificant. And Sartre will say that the other is a pure hole in the world—a most noteworthy insight, but he stops his analysis too soon. The other proceeds from the absolutely absent. His

relationship with the absolutely absent from which he comes *does not indicate, does not reveal* this absent; and yet the absent has a meaning in a face. This signifyingness is not a way for the absent to be given in a blank in the presence of a face—which would bring us back to a mode of disclosure" (Lévinas 1998, pp. 102–3)

11 "Duty or responsibility binds me to the other, to the other as other, and ties me in my absolute singularity to the other as other. God is the name of the absolute other as other and as unique" (Derrida 2002, p. 68).

Reference List

Arendt H. (1968). *Men in Dark Times*. San Diego: Harcourt Brace & Company.
Arendt H. (1998). *The Human Condition*. Chicago: University of Chicago Press.
Cavaleri P. (2001). "Dal campo al confine di contatto. Contributo per una riconsiderazione del confine di contatto in psicoterapia della Gestalt." In M. Spagnuolo Lobb (ed.) *La psicoterapia della Gestalt. Ermeneutica e clinica*. Milan: FrancoAngeli.
Cavaleri P. (2003). *La profondità della superficie. Percorsi introduttivi alla psicoterapia della Gestalt*. Milan: FrancoAngeli.
Derrida J. (1995) *The Gift of Death*. Translated by David Wills. Chicago/London: The University of Chicago Press. Translated in Italian as *Donare la morte*. Milan: Jaca Book, 2002.
Devereux G. (1980). *Basic Problems of Ethnopsychiatry*. Chicago: University of Chicago Press.
Francesetti G. (2016). "You Cry, I Feel Pain". The Emerging, Co-created Self as the Foundation of Anthropology, Psychopathology and Treatment in Gestalt Therapy. In J.-M. Robine (ed.) *Self. A Polyphony of Contemporary Gestalt Therapists*. St. Romain-La-Virvée: L'Exprimerie.
Francesetti G., Gecele M. (2009). "A Gestalt Therapy Perspective on Psychopathology and Diagnosis." *British Gestalt Journal* 18, 2, 5–20.
Gecele M. (2014). "Introduzione ai disturbi di personalità. Considerazioni diagnostiche e sociali." In G. Francesetti, M. Gecele, J. Roubal (eds.) *La psicoterapia della Gestalt nella pratica clinica. Dalla psicopatologia all'estetica del contatto*. Milan: FrancoAngeli.
Gecele M. (2019). "Chasing Joy in the Liquid Time of Emptiness: Obsessive Compulsive Experiences." In G. Francestti, E. Kerry Reed, C. Vazquez Bandin (eds.), *Obsessive Compulsive Experiences: a Gestalt Therapy Perspective*. Madrid: Los Libros del CTP.
Gecele M., Francesetti G. (2007) "The Polis as the Ground and Horizon of Therapy." In G. Francesetti (ed.), *Panic Attacks and Postmodernity. Gestalt Therapy Between Clinical and Social Perspectives*. Milan: FrancoAngeli, pp. 170–209. Originally published as "La polis come 'ground' e orizzonte della terapia. In G. Francesetti (ed.) *Attacchi di panico e postmodernità, la psicoterapia della Gestalt fra clinica e società*. Milan: FrancoAngeli, 2005.
Lotman Ju. (1976), "Culture and Information" [Introduction to Ju. Lotman's Studies in the Typology of Culture (Tartu, 1970), pp. 3–6. Translated by Stephen White.] *Dispositio*. Vol. 1 No. 3 (1976): 213–215.
Merleau-Ponty M. (2012). *Phenomenology of Perception*. Translated by Donald A. Landes. Oxon, UK: Routledge. Translated in Italian as *Fenomenologia della percezione*. Milan: Bompiani, 2005.

Perls F.S., Hefferline R.F., Goodman P. (1994). *Gestalt Therapy. Excitement and Growth in the Human Personality*. Gouldsboro ME: The Gestalt Journal Press. Translated in Italian as *Teoria e pratica della terapia della Gestalt*. Rome: Astrolabio, 1971.

Remotti F. (2006). "Il pregio di ciò che manca e la laicità degli altri." In G. Preterossi (ed.) *Le ragioni dei laici*. Rome/Bari: Laterza.

Riva F. (1999). *Il pensiero dell'altro (E. Lévinas, G. Marcel, P. Ricoeur)*. Rome: Edizioni Lavoro.

Salonia G. (1999). "Dialogare nel tempo della frammentazione." In F. Rametta, M. Naro (ed.) *Impense Adlaboravit*. Palermo: Facoltà Teologica di Sicilia.

Salonia G. (2000). "La criminalità giovanile tra vecchie e nuove regole. Verso l'integrazione dello straniero nella polis." *Quaderni di Gestalt* XX, 30/31, 100–108.

Salonia G. (2001). "Tempo e relazione. L'intenzionalità relazionale come orizzonte ermeneutica della psicoterapia della Gestalt." In M. Spagnuolo Lobb (ed.) *La psicoterapia della Gestalt. Ermeneutica e clinica*. Milan: FrancoAngeli.

Salonia G. (2007). *Odòs*. Bologna: EDB.

Salonia G. (2004). *Sulla felicità e dintorni. Tra corpo, tempo e parola*. Ragusa: ARGO Edizioni.

Sichera A. (2001). "A confronto con Gadamer: per una epistemologia ermeneutica della Gestalt." In M. Spagnuolo Lobb (ed.) *La psicoterapia della Gestalt. Ermeneutica e clinica*. Milan: FrancoAngeli.

Spagnuolo Lobb M. (ed.) (2001a). *La psicoterapia della Gestalt. Ermeneutica e clinica*. Milan: FrancoAngeli.

Spagnuolo Lobb M. (2004). "L'awareness dans la pratique post-moderne de la gestalt-thérapie." *Gestalt* XV, 27, 41–58.

Spagnuolo Lobb M., Amendt-Lyon N. (ed.) (2007). *Il permesso di creare. l'arte della psicoterapia della Gestalt*. Milan: FrancoAngeli.

Spagnuolo Lobb M. (2007a). "La relazione terapeutica nell'approccio gestaltico." In P. Petrini, A. Zucconi (eds.) *La relazione che cura*. Rome: Alpes Italia, pp. 527–536.

5 Narrating, Communicating, and Translating

Hermeneutics and translation processes

Just as there exist utopias of ideal places, eras, and relationships, so too there exist linguistic utopias. Such utopias seek to erase the wounds of otherness, guided by a desire for total communication and understanding—a desire to return to a hypothetical age of humanity 'before Babel.' These utopias are laid bare by the translation process.

> [...] Walter Benjamin (1923)[1] said that translation implies a pure language, a *reine Sprache*. Since the translated text can never reproduce the meaning of the original, we have to rely on the feeling that all languages somehow converge. All languages—each taken as a whole—intend one and the same thing, which, however, is not accessible to any one of them but only to the totality of their mutually complementary intentions: "If there is a language of truth, in which the final secrets that draw the effort of all thinking are held in silent repose, then this language of truth is true language. And it is precisely this language—to glimpse or describe it is the only perfection the philosopher can hope for—that is concealed, intensively, in translations."[2] [...] Now, it is beneficial for a translator to think that his or her desire to translate springs from this wish to grasp God's own thinking, but since this is a very private inner feeling (and there is no public way of verifying God's thoughts), can we use it as an inter-subjective criterion to assess the degree to which a translation is successful?
>
> (Eco 2001, pp. 10–11)

Language is body, relationship, and transcendence. In order to communicate, for language to become narrative, an 'other than oneself' is necessary; it is necessary to set into motion multiple translation processes. Every relational phenomenon is, in a certain sense, a translation. This underlines and, at the same time, 'resolves' the problem of grounds, pointing to the existence of an irrepressible difference and to the need to undertake a path to communicate and approach the other. A goal that is unachievable, yet necessary at the same

DOI: 10.4324/9781003568292-5

time. "Being this way for all of human life, so it is for speaking, writing, reading, and translating. Just as saying something implies essentially forgoing saying everything, all that man does and that always occurs only within the partiality of inevitable choices or preferences takes place in the shadows within the limitations of the human condition" (Razza 2001, p. 18, my translation). No translation can be done without being at the boundary and being open to new languages, to the other, without the intersecting of grounds in which there is already the possibility of otherness.

> According to Lotman, it is clear that the value of communication does not lie in what is held in common at the outset but in the possibility of bringing face-to-face the respective diversities, memories, and languages that are not shared. As the Russian scholar puts it, the paradox is that the value of communication lies in what makes it so hard, bordering on impossible, because it is in such a situation that the need arises to "translate the untranslatable," thereby generating new culture.
> (Pezzini & Sedda, my translation)

Translation comes before language. It comes from the ground and it transforms it, without fixing it too rigidly. It is the opposite of fundamentalism, which fixes the figure rigidly while neglecting the ground.

> "The translated text must, anticipating a response, conserve within itself an element of transference into the other language. Otherwise dialogue is not possible."[3] Texts that transmute from one culture to another are transformed, bearing in them the traces of the pathways and journeys they have made; it is their adaptability that allows exchange and enrichment.
> (Pezzini & Sedda, my translation)

Every interpretation, every narrative of contexts and societies constructed by sociologists, anthropologists, and psychologists can be reinterpreted and re-read as being part and parcel of the same culture of which they are a critical tool. They are stories within stories, a hermeneutic circle. Every interpretation is an articulation of a context, but it opens up to diverse possibilities, as happens in any translation process. In dealing with multiple and complex grounds and fostering their possibility of being fertile, translation processes are important (Giaccardi 2005). It is a specific and complex mode of creative adjustment. Translation means preceding the figure of the sentence, connecting up with the ground from which it emerges.

> Translatability is an essential quality of certain works, which is not to say that it is essential for the works themselves that they be translated; it means, rather, that a specific significance inherent in the original manifests itself in its translatability. [...] no translation would be possible if in its

ultimate essence it strove for likeness to the original. For in its afterlife—which could not be called that if it were not a transformation and a renewal of something living—the original undergoes a change.

(Benjamin 1968, pp. 71–73)

Translation in psychotherapy

In the early days of the history of psychotherapy, at the dawning of psychoanalysis, it was thought that the 'translation' of the individual in the world, seen as adjustment to society via an analytic process, was one-directional—from the unconscious to the conscious—and predetermined, a process of progressive and faithful clarification and illumination. Today we have come, through various stages, to a situation in which relational and communicative processes form a web of multidirectional vectors. 'Truth' is created through the contact process itself, providing there is a third element to assure against madness and self-referentiality.

> Social disintegration can provoke the disorientation of the subject, who always needs to come face-to-face with an other in order to construct and define themself. One of the riskiest outcomes of disintegration is when it takes the form of the internal fragmentation of the subject's meanings, which are no longer drawn together into unity and utterability, due to the lack of a relationship that activates processes for deciphering and sharing experiences. [...] The other, even if he lives next to me, inhabits a universe of meanings that is different to mine. Not only does he have his own experience and judgment of the world, but he uses the same words with different connotations and even denotations. If attention is not paid to such complexity, if the appropriate time is not given to the premises themselves of communication, equivocation, misunderstanding, and an escalating disintegration await. These days, the American wishing to engage with another American needs to pay almost the same attention to cultural diversity demanded of the anthropologist who comes into contact with an indigenous community of Africa or Amazonia.
>
> (Salonia 1999, pp. 574–575, my translation)

In a fragmented and multiethnic context, it is essential to find the words to express one's experiences, discomforts, and joys, and to communicate them. More important still is to acquire the ability to listen and to let the other's experience resound in you. The image is that of a tower of Babel, where the sense of what one feels, speaks, and communicates is constructed in an impossible, yet necessary dialogue. Only if there is a relationship, an intentionality directed at encounter, is the possibility opened not just for communication, but for existence. Translatability, like relationships, implies the recognition of otherness—the difficulty of reaching the other and being reached by it—and, at the same time, the search for a language to reach the other.

> According to him [Schleiermacher], a translation can move in either of two directions: either the author is brought to the language of the reader, or the reader is carried to the language of the author. In the first case, we do not translate, in the proper sense of the word; we, in fact, do an imitation, or a paraphrase of the original text. It is only when we force the reader from his linguistic habits and oblige him to move within those of the author that there is actually translation.
> (Ortega y Gasset 1992, p. 108)

If your existence does not concern me, if it does not resound in mine, and, at the same time, if it is not something other to me, we cannot communicate. Listening and seeking to understand sets into motion a translation process. Otherness and relationships come before us; 'we' comes before 'I' (Salonia 1989). The third element is the hiatus that stops fusion, preventing contact from being reified and losing its meaning. The fullness of encounter does not lie in the fusion of an 'us' but in a time and place to be reached through the rhythmic progression of the relationship. Reaching for contact implies the acceptance of otherness, whose manifestations, by definition, cannot be known in advance.

Power and translatability

As therapists, we are situated within cultural processes that are also historical processes and power processes, which cannot fail to be part of our foreknowledge. We start from a defined, partial point of view, drawing from a ground, the awareness of which is essential. Always bearing in mind the possibility and existence of an 'other' point of view allows us to avoid both the risk of follie a deux and the imbalance created by a relationship founded on power.

> A) First of all, it is necessary to clarify who the subjects involved in translation are, starting from the premise that it is unlikely that they will be on the same level. B) Consequently, it is necessary to ask ourselves what their relations are in terms of strength, power, prestige, and authoritativeness (which do not always coincide). C) Third, it is pertinent to ask ourselves whether all the subjects involved are interested in engaging in translation transactions, bearing in mind that there may be subjects interested in translating their own culture into other cultures, but not in the reverse transaction. As was said earlier (§2), for there to be cultural translation, it is necessary that there be subjects interested in such a transaction, who "decide" to make it, who "make an effort" to accomplish it, and who "choose" how to do it. In other words, between two or more cultures, a translation

does not come about by chance, nor by necessity; there needs to be a "culture" of cultural translation.

(Remotti 2009, p. 102, my translation)

The fact of originating in a circumscribed space-time culture does not prevent certain values, principles, and concepts from being elements of the boundary, able to overflow a cultural sphere and be enriched and transformed in other contexts. When the sphere of reference is the transcultural field, any theoretical perspective—which emerges and develops in specific times and specific places—comes up against the contradiction of trying to describe something of which it is a product. It is true that psychotherapy belongs to the history of the 'western' world and to move beyond it, it has to find a way to cross its boundaries; but it is also true that its history is a story of boundaries in which the polarities of uniformity/discontinuity, centre/margins, particular/general play a significant role. Different schools and currents have emerged and developed in attunement or in opposition to their relative contexts, engaging with aspects and articulations of society. There are many boundaries, both concentric and intersecting. It is not always easy to see when you are crossing one, if you are participating in a transformative process, or if, instead, there has been no real movement.

In communicative and relational processes, as psychotherapy, hermeneutics, and translation are at different levels, sense and direction are decentred, shifted forever beyond, towards an external point to be reached. In the epistemological principles of Gestalt therapy, though they originated in a precise space-time context, there is already an inherent inclination towards the external, towards otherness. The approach is of a hermeneutic kind and the forms attributed to experience by the theory are the fruit of a dialogical relationship with society. Their translatability derives from that, as does one of the premises underpinning this book—the idea that Gestalt therapy is a helpful tool for understanding multicultural contexts and for constructing an intercultural agenda. Naturally, in turn, the theoretical framework is transformed through its own workings. Every discipline is transformed and enriched when it moves beyond the culture that produced it.

Complexity and boundaries

In cases where the cultural space acquires a territorial connotation, the boundary takes on a literally spatial sense and acts as a "buffer" mechanism. The boundary is also well represented by specific social figures, such as, in the pre-modern tradition, the executioner, the miller, or the witch doctor, who dwelled, most significantly, on the margins of the territory, at the boundary between the cultural world and the mythological world, and hence in belonging at the same time to two worlds (life/death, nature/

culture, human/divine...), they served as privileged agents of translation. [...] Today it could be said that it is the media system, or its mythology at least, that poses itself, through figures like the journalist, the reporter, the correspondent, the commentator, as a great and widespread translation system and filter (of mediation) between semiospheres of different "personality." [...] Therefore, from the point of view of its imminent functioning, the boundary unites two different semiotic spheres, but from the point of view of their reciprocal self-description, it divides them; having self-consciousness in the semiotic cultural relationship means being conscious of one's own specificity, of one's being a counterpoint to other spheres.
(Pezzini & Sedda, my translation)

Going back to what was said in the chapter 'Invisible Grounds,' we can think of the journalist, the anthropologist, and the psychotherapist as boundary figures. They are figures that dwell on the margins, where not only culture is milled—think of the role of the miller—and reworked, but also where differences stand out the most, and can therefore truly encounter each other; where processes of translation, of incessant construction and transformation are active; where grounds intersect, making ever-new and surprising figures possible. If therapists become entrenched and too rigid in one vision of the world, they divest themselves of their role, of the potential to be a sensor, a translator, and a transducer. Continuous effort and attention are needed to be constantly sensitive to macroscopic and microscopic changes in the context.

The permeability of the boundary is tied to the instability of the periphery, which is bilingual by nature. It tends to aggressively oppose the centre, where, throughout the nineteenth century at least, culturally dominant institutions were organized, which can be seen, for example, in the organization of the urban area or, more generally, the territory. From this perspective, the boundary takes on the configuration of an actual space in an ever-more decisive way. A place where the mixing of languages can set into gear, through their deconstruction and "primitivization," processes of creolization and self-redenomination that foster the creation of new languages and new communities.
(cf. Fabbri 2003,[4] quoted in Pezzini & Sedda, my translation)

Instable and bilingual, the periphery opposes the centre—or centres—and encourages deconstruction and redenomination processes. It permits evolutionary change; it is the life blood and nourishing ground—given by possibilities that are present and imminent, but not given—that makes life and growth possible. The commixture of languages is always fertile, indicating and leading to an elsewhere, but also to continuous interaction and integration with the ground.

Notes

1 Benjamin W. (1923). "Die Aufgabe des Übersetzers" [The Task of the Translator] in *Charles Baudelaire, "Tableaux parisiens": Deutsche Übertragung mit einem Vorwort über die Aufgabe des Übersetzers, von Walter Benjamin.*
2 Eco U. (1993). *La ricerca della lingua perfetta nella cultura europea.* Laterza, Rome-Bari. Translated into English by James Fentress as *The Search for the Perfect Language.* Oxford, UK/Cambridge, USA: Blackwell, 1995.
3 Lotman J.M. (1985). *La semiosfera.* Marsilio, Venice, 68. Translated from the Russian by Wilma Clark as "On the Semiosphere." In *Signs Systems Studies* 33.1, 2005: 205–229; p. 218.
4 Fabbri, P. (2003). *Elogio di Babele,* Rome: Meltemi.

References

Benjamin W. (1968) *Illuminations.* Translated by Harry Zohn. New York: Harcourt, Brace & World.
Eco U. (2001). *Experiences in Translation.* Translated by Alistair McEwan. Toronto/Buffalo/London: University of Toronto Press.
Giaccardi C. (2005). *La comunicazione interculturale.* Bologna: Il Mulino.
Ortega y Gasset J. (1992) "The Misery and the Splendour of Translation." Translated by Elizabeth Gamble Miller. In R. Schulte, J. Biguenet (eds.), *Theories of Translation: An Anthology of Essays from Dryden to Derrida.* Chicago/London: University of Chicago Press, 1992, pp. 93–112.
Pezzini I., Sedda F. *Semiosfera,* www.culturalstudies.it/dizionario.
Razza C. (2001). "La sconfitta del luogo comune. Ortega e la traduzione." In J. Ortega y Gasset *Miseria e splendore della traduzione.* Genoa: Il melangolo, pp. 7–25.
Remotti F. (2009). "Tradurre e convivere. L'antropologo e il diritto interculturale." *Daimon. Annuario di diritto comparato delle religioni* 8, 97–108.
Salonia G. (1999). "Dialogare nel tempo della frammentazione." In F. Rametta, M. Naro (ed.) *Impense Adlaboravit.* Palermo: Facoltà Teologica di Sicilia.
Salonia G. (1989). "Dal Noi all'Io-Tu: contributo per una teoria evolutiva del contatto." *Quaderni di Gestalt* V, 8/9, 45–54.

6 Linguistic Grounds
Bringing Reality to Life

Corporeity, complexity, and incompleteness of speech

Poetry in all its forms is, in practice, the only instance of self-referential speech. The words of a poem do not refer to any ulterior meaning, but have significance in themselves; they have meaning and significance in so far as they are spoken. Speech really is the thing in poetry and nothing can ever be understood of it by those who interpret it as a sign of an unknown unconscious or the law in view of a biography, without listening in silence to its voice and mystery. Neither we nor the poet need to know the latent content of the symbol.

(Sichera 2001, p. 38, my translation)

Surprise! Language does not consist simply of the content it conveys. Communication does not just concern the figure, it is not just grammatical logic. Even without translation, in speaking different idioms, we communicate and understand something. The human voice itself produces physical and psychological effects—vibrations, movements in vital signs. Every language, even if foreign, is a human language and it resounds in every one of us. In reality, this is no big surprise, but is it not so trivial if we stop and think, feel, and talk about it, as we are doing in this book.

Silences, rests, rhythm, and intonation are all part of a language. Speech is connected to breathing and in Gestalt therapy the therapeutic relationship is attentive to restoring the potentiality of this vital function, which supports experience through continuous exchange with the exterior. Language originates from the body and is a part of it, but it is also situated 'in-between' the organism and the environment. It has a sense of direction because there is an interlocutor who comes before it, an 'other than me' to be reached or who wishes to reach me, in a never-ending effort that is never exhausted. The plurality of languages is both the concrete experience of and metaphor for communication that never reaches a definitive destination, but continuously builds bridges and relationships, spanning distance and proximity.

DOI: 10.4324/9781003568292-6

Reading comes from reading out aloud, often collectively. Poetry, above all, is and remains speech, to be uttered and listened to, expressing bodily power and giving voice to a collective dimension—the dimension expressed by the chorus in Greek tragedy. In all the great religious traditions, the physical power of speech constructs connections between narration, performance, rite, and presence.

> The fact is that the stupendous reality, which is language, will not be understood at its root if one does not begin by noticing that speech is composed above all of silences. A person incapable of quieting many things would not be capable of talking. And each language is a different equation of statements and silences. All peoples silence some things in order to be able to say others. Otherwise, everything would be unsayable.
> (Ortega y Gasset 1992, p. 104)

The 'foreigner'—someone who dwells in a different language—can encourage us to pause, to stop and listen to our own voice and to others', opening each word up and unhinging it. On the contrary, too many stimuli, too many words disconnected from experience, without an address and addressee, take power away from speech itself. The figure stands out less clearly.

Speaking about language is a fundamental passage in the discourse on otherness, diversity, and relationships. A crossroads of complexity and multiple grounds underpin the power and limits of language—its incompleteness and implicit yearning for something that can never be completely accomplished. Knowing the pain of inexpressibility and total non-correspondence is one of the stages in the formation of culture.

Literature, linguistics, philosophy, anthropology, semiotics, psychology, sociology, religion, poetry, and cinema; psychology and psychotherapy: All the disciplines connected with language are, in their turn, languages—or metalanguages—that are inter-translatable, enriching each other and creating new experiences and new information. In our day and age, the quest for knowledge increasingly journeys into the interstices between different fields of learning. When it lingers in these intermediate spaces, even elements that, confined within a discipline, seemed incapable of bearing fruit can become new, stimulating, and fertile, when seen from another perspective and connected with other fields of learning. Just like in the encounter between cultures, which gives rise to cultures themselves. Words are also a locus of ethics, a field from which a slight yet robust relational and social thread unravels, allowing us to find further connections between language and psychotherapy.

> Communication is the basis on which networks of belonging are built up and consolidated, together with the locus of the polis. At the same time, it is also the tool with which we can redefine the limits and confines of a truly private locus, namely the oikos. In this light, Jürgen Habermas' definition

of communication as the ethical action par excellence proves to be particularly pregnant with meaning for our contemporary context.

(Gecele & Francesetti 2007, pp. 206–207).

Ground and direction

Language is thus a figure constructed from scratch in every single experience, in the here and now of every relationship. However, we can also consider language as ground, as a support that exists before us and transcends us, that speaks to being and draws from it. Silence and speech stand in a reciprocal and shifting relationship, transmuting continuously from figure to ground and ground to figure. "The quest for an absolute, for a language that is as expressive, as dense with meaning, and as originary as possible, becomes an uninterrupted hermeneutical quest: truth as quest for truth, for an agreement of the real with mutability and, at the same time, with an extreme abstraction" (Heidegger 1973, p. 105, my translation from the Italian translation of the German).

Originary reality to be made to emerge, novelty to be created. How are these two, apparently polarized, modes integrated? Speech is, at once, retraced and invented anew each and every time, on a pathway paved with age-old stratifications. This happens in everyday adult experiences, but also in developmental stages. Every infant traces out a path, starting from a mother language and a father language, bringing together two worlds and creating them.

> The most important achievement of expression is not to commit to writing some thoughts that might otherwise be lost; a writer hardly ever rereads his own works and, on the first reading, a great work deposits in us everything that we will subsequently draw from it. The operation of expression, when successful, does not simply leave to the reader or the writer himself a reminder; it makes the signification exist as a thing at the very heart of the text, it brings it to life in an organism of words, it installs this signification in the writer or the reader like a new sense organ, and it opens a new field or a new dimension to our experience.
>
> (Merleau-Ponty 2012, p. 188)

Reproduction, discovery, and creation of language

A childhood solitude, a lack of sharing, recognition, and support in feeling and giving a name to feeling has major repercussions on the construction of language, which risks being sterile and empty, lifeless, without any correspondence to experience (Perls et al. 1994). Even in these cases, however, language can be re-found and reinvented in adulthood, with the support of other relationships.

In Daniel Stern's theory of infant development (Stern 1985), we find fulcrums of experience called the *verbal self* and the *narrative self*—two modes of what he calls "senses of self."[2] These senses of self originate in specific stages of development and then continue to mark out growth lines, which intersect with those that come later, without being cancelled by them.

The verbal self develops in close contact with the intersubjective self. It emerges within the relationship with the mother or other significant caregivers, arising from the infant's sense of certainty that the mother 'knows' the names of things. It is the sharing of a secret—the appellation, magical in its way, to be given to an object, an experience, an emotion. This brings us close to the creator word, to the God that names things and reveals those names to humankind, giving knowledge of them and power over them. This shows us all the creative power that lies in language. A power that reveals itself all the more with the emergence and development of the narrative self. This fulcrum implicitly contains a third element, the narrative itself, which was not yet found in the verbal self. The development of language thus brings us back to triality, from a developmental perspective. In this case, the third element is first of all language itself, but the father, the family, the affiliation group are also third elements. Through the developmental process, the infant acquires a competence and relational maturity that implies the capability of dwelling at boundaries, of being exposed to life and feeling the wound of absence. A world is structured in which the story of that life unfolds and in which language itself acquires meaning. Access to language is neither creation nor follie à deux, but a continuous and strenuous process of translation, an attempt to articulate and construct the world, and to reach the other. "I relate something to you; I relate myself to you." Progressively, the bonds constructed around linguistic exchanges extend to new people and to new contexts.

Language has the power to include or exclude, to define experiences, abstractions, and forms of relationships. Bonds, loyalties, and memory are expressed forcefully in language and narrative.

Linguistic creative adjustment

The power of speech is a form of creative adjustment. It attempts to contain, to fix in time and in space, what incessantly flows. However, it also alludes to the indefinite, to the unspeakable, to what is not yet present. It is the possibility of grasping the creativity and freshness of every new encounter, of every new start, as well as the potentiality that lies in listening to the pre-existent, to origins, to meaning. It is not just contact with different languages that causes language to change. The unstable equilibrium between structural rigidities and adjustment possibilities evolves above all with the profound and continuous changes of life. "Although the need to pin down the world is fundamental, also for the purposes of communication, the impossibility of truly fixing it is strongly felt in the construction of language, which only this way manages to remain close to the intimacy of originary experience" (Razza 2001, p. 22, my translation). Sometimes, language is a place in which to hide away and avoid contact, a space of make-believe and inauthenticity. Dissolving this superstructure requires relational support, because it entails going through the pain of a story, of more than one story, embodied in flesh. Such phenomena can be part of any person's experience, but they are made all the more acute and amplified by migration processes, by situations in which exchanges, passages, and changes are greater, but also where rigid fixations and cancellations are possible, through to a forced and empty plurilingualism.

Speech in human experience and transcendence

What we are saying is that, on the way towards listening to otherness, we come across a variety of languages. If we stop and gain experience of them, we can hear them resound in us, because every word, every accent, no matter how foreign, alludes to life and to humanity. Language does not just have denotative value. It echoes with stories, passions, yearning, bodies, and earth, embodying them.

Many religious traditions hold language to be sacred, referring to a single, specific language or to speech itself. Focusing on the three monotheistic religions, in Judaism and in Islam it is the original language of the holy texts that is held to be sacred; Christianity is instead multilingual, and in its claim to universalism revolves around the translatable word. Thus, sacredness extends to the translation. Multiplicity and uniqueness echo in each other.

These three religions are based on a truth built on a Thou or a He, not an I. Thus they bear within themselves both the potentials—of questioning themselves as individuals—and the risks—of absolutizing their own point of view, transposing it externally—given by the continuous reference to an elsewhere. And the word of their respective sacred texts bears the same potentials and risks—it can dislodge and bring renewal, but it can also take on the rigidity and dangerousness of a weapon.

In the religious sphere, in much the same way as in other human contexts, the word is a go-between, a means and instrument, but also ground, third element, and containment. As we can see by looking at the Jewish tradition, for example, in the following quote.

> [T]he link between God and man is not an emotional communion that takes place within the love of a God incarnate, but a spiritual or intellectual [*esprits*] relationship which takes place through an education in the Torah. It is precisely a word, not incarnate, from God that ensures a living God among us. Confidence in a God Who is not made manifest through any worldly authority can rely only on internal evidence and the values of an education. To the credit of Judaism, there is nothing blind about this. This accounts for the monologue's closing remark, in which Yossel ben Yossel echoes the whole of the Torah: 'I love him, but I love even more his Torah… And even if I were deceived by him and became

disillusioned, I should nevertheless observe the precepts of the Torah.' Is this blasphemy? At the very least, it is a protection against the madness of a direct contact with the Sacred that is unmediated by reason. But above all it is a confidence that does not rely on the triumph of any institution, it is the internal evidence of morality supplied by the Torah.
(Lévinas 1990, p. 144)

These words powerfully stress how the Thou—in religion, as in human relationships—can become a mirror of the I, transforming faith into idolatry and the relationship into a motionless unity in which all otherness vanishes. Lévinas tells us how the law, the written word, protects against the inherent risks of a direct, unmediated relationship with the divine.

Names

There are many connections between speech and sacred spheres, and also between speech and a mythological dimension that is choral and timeless.

Therefore mythological description is monolinguistic in principle: the world's objects are described by means of this very same world, which is structured in the same way. However, nonmythological description is definitely polylinguistic: reference to metalanguage is important precisely as reference to a different language; it does not matter whether the metalanguage is a language of abstract constructs or a foreign language, since what is important is the process itself of translation and interpretation.
(Lotman & Uspenskij 1977, pp. 233–234)

'Proper' names fall within this definition of mythological language. More generally, they fall within the crossroads between the human and the sacred, between individual and world. They connect ground and figure, identifying the single individual, but also situating where they each belong. They evoke a linguistic world. They evoke and allude.

Let's go back to the original act of naming things, recalling the countless speakable and unspeakable names of God found at the heart of many religious traditions.

The deepest images of this divine word and the point where human language participates most intimately in the divine infinity of the pure word, the point at which it cannot become finite word and knowledge, are the human name. The theory of proper names is the theory of the frontier between finite and infinite language. Of all beings, man is the only one who names his own kind, as he is the only one whom God did not name. […] By giving names, parents dedicate their children to God; the names they give do not correspond—in a metaphysical rather than etymological sense—to any knowledge, for they name newborn children. In a strict sense, no name ought (in its etymological meaning) to correspond to any person, for the proper name is the word of God in human sounds. By it each man is guaranteed his creation by God, and in this sense he is himself creative, as is expressed by mythological wisdom in the idea (which doubtless not infrequently comes true) that a man's name is his fate. The proper name is the communion of man with the *creative* word of God.

(Benjamin 1986, pp. 323–324)

Walter Benjamin's words, which come from a Judeo-Christian horizon, pave the way for us to listen to other words, words brought by Lucien Hounkpatin to Italy in 2002 at a conference in Turin,[3] which evoke a multiplicity of worlds, in a web of connections. Let's listen to how every infant makes its entrance into a polycentric order, where nothing is taken for granted and the risks are many; where there are no truths to be revealed and the individual is completely absorbed by a network of connections, both determined and random.

We have a foundational god, one we are then not concerned with. There are no shrines to him. He is out there somewhere, but we are not concerned with him. What he did was to create a multiplicity of deities that, regardless of belief, have functional roles. So there is a parley of many deities, who do not all speak the same language (bear in mind that the deities are, by their nature, belligerent among themselves). There is, however, one deity, who is materially poor but extraordinarily rich in his function, which is language—language to try and communicate, mediate, and translate the things of the other deities, so as to connect them all to each other. That is why the two main functions of the Fathers of Mysteries, the *babalawos*, are: translate, translate, translate ... and complexify, complexify, complexify, to gather the substance of the considerations. That means that when a person is born into this complexity and multiplicity of deities and into this profusion of elements that then constitute him/her, his or her nature, his or her identity, needs to be determined. The individual is understood, in this world, as a person who inherits elements from the cosmos—elements that "make" him/her, the heritage of both his/her lineage and the deities who constitute his/her world. [...] Therefore, these multiple elements that determine the hidden identity of the individual start interacting in infancy, specifically from its "nomination," from the first word that nominates the event, from the moment of pregnancy. I will give you an idea of how the identity of things is constructed. From the moment the pregnancy event is known, words are not delivered everywhere, nor are they said to just anyone. The future parents, proud of the event, have to deliver the first words to their parents, the future grandparents, and the role of the future grandparents is to go and see the *babalawo* to deliver, in their turn, the words to him. In the Western world, it would be like asking the future mother to go to her parents, and asking her parents to take her directly to the therapist. After that, it is as though a first shell of containment were constituted around the family, or the future family. Through divination, the *babalawo*, seeks to grasp the roles of each person with respect to the event and to understand the event's relationship with the space of the invisible, or hidden space. It is about gauging the elements of the child's "being," not the future person he or she will become. But once things have been delivered, and the word has been spread, saying things assumes the utmost importance. How is the word spread? First we think of the intimate, then we move from the intimate to the private, and then from the private to the social. The intimate is what the parents experience; the private is given by delivering that to the grandparents, with the support of the *babalawo*, and the public is the "outside." [...] So, behind the nomination of a child, for instance as "crying baby," there is no assignment, but the construction of a frame around the child, in which and through which people, and not only the parents, can nurture the child. It involves listening to the child's crying, being able to say something about his or her crying. Only after that can the frame be opened up and the step can be made from "crying baby" to the notion of "calm baby." [...] What we seek to do is say that every child is different and we are on a multiple pathway, where it is not about doing good or doing harm, but knowing how to nurture each child in his or her singularity and originality.

(Hounkpatin 2002, pp. 51–54, my translation)

Cultural anthropology teaches us that stages of passage in the life cycle can involve a change of proper name and the determination of new status through the attribution of collective names (Geertz 1973; Baxter & Almagor 1978; Bernardi 1984). Thus, multiple names mark changes and discontinuity for the person, while, vice versa, a same name can identify an entire group. This horizon opens up perspectives that lead to multiple narratives of journeys and stories, both individual and collective.

Many rituals are founded on the power of speech and names. Practices of magical value, and hence of connection—the individual to the group, humans to nature, nature to the supernatural—have also emerged and developed along the boundaries in the encounter between monotheisms and previous traditions, in various parts of the world (Nathan & Stengers 1996; Beneduce 1998; Moro & Revah-Levy 1998). Using a language, dwelling in it, also means opening up these worlds.

Language as constriction

For an immigrant, or for a wayfarer who does not dwell in the land of their native language, there is an ambivalence in every linguistic act. To learn or not to learn a new language and use it to express concepts, thoughts, sentiments, and emotions? To preserve or not to preserve the memory of age-old sounds? To feel the constriction to use originary words, or to shrug it off?

Encounters between different languages—in one and the same person who speaks more than one language, or between people who speak different languages—are fertile if they unfold within a horizon of responsibility and freedom, which is creative and creating. They become pathological, in the sense of reduction, loss, and absence, when relational, social, and political dynamics determine an asymmetry and bring about creative adjustments that are not constructive and phenomena such as semilingualism.[4] It is important to bear in mind these various possibilities also within therapy work, when clients find themselves in a linguistic setting that is not their original one.

> The possibility of speaking his mother tongue is therefore a strong sign of acknowledgement of the patient's cultural heritage and acknowledgement of the fact that the patient's history begins much earlier than his birth and his migration. It is the acknowledgement of the historical course of his genealogy, of the importance of the earliest traces and earliest events of life for understanding the present pain of the patient and the disorder dwelling in him. It is not about resorting to a fossilized mother tongue, but about permitting the patient to use this tool or just say certain words in his mother tongue, so as not to bar the way to other possible worlds. It is the patient who will structure any such recourse to his mother tongue and the passages between the languages that dwell in him; because what is sure is that just as we dwell in a language, so it dwells in us, in what is a necessarily interactive process.
> (Moro & Revah-Levy 1998, p. 121, my translation)

Bilingualism and life cycle

What is the experience of an adult who learns a new language? And that of a child who lives in a country where the language spoken is different to the parents' language—a child whose parents often do not know the names of things? In learning a new language, or more than one language simultaneously, that child will structure another world, other worlds that are more or less complete, welcoming, or threatening. Different ways of telling the same story may intertwine or take parallel courses, whose paths are unlikely to meet. Individual words will have a different pregnancy in each of the languages.

Learning a new language as an adult is different from learning it as a child. And learning one is different when it is out of an interest in knowledge, or for professional reasons, or as part of a migration process. Living in an 'other' linguistic setting can lead to an exacerbation of renunciative modes and make it harder to perceive and express a need, demonstrate a skill, or manifest a drive. If the language of reference is muted, this changes the framework of meanings in which a person lives and constructs the meaning of their own life; it changes the world. Passageways are gone through, junctions crossed. Contents and experiences move from a known, age-old narrative to a new narrative; speech and individual words develop together, without order of priority.

Words may be less pregnant with meaning than in the native language, but they may also be more pregnant when the new language emerges as part of a strong need for expression and contact. The two languages, the two worlds, come together, unfolding in parallel without being able to meet, or interacting in a constructive or destructive way.

> It should be recalled that in the assimilation of any natural language, there are two methods for its teaching. The first follows the teaching of the native language or the early teaching of a foreign language. In this case, no rules of any kind are introduced into the learner's consciousness; they are replaced by texts. The child memorizes numerous usages and on the basis of them learns to generate texts by himself. The second method is enacted when determinate rules are introduced into the learner's consciousness and on the basis of them he can generate texts by himself. Furthermore, although in the former case the texts are introduced into the learner's consciousness, in practice they immediately rise in rank to act as metatexts, or exemplars. [...] The introduction of grammatical rules in the individual's memory presupposes a certain linguistic mastery, whereas teaching by means of texts can occur on virgin soil. Accordingly, use is generally made of rules when teaching a foreign language to adult people, and of texts when teaching children even their native language. Thus both of these two ways of constructing the cultural code can be considered stages of a single evolution that takes place through the alternation of different constitutive principles.
> (Lotman & Uspenskij 2001, p. 69, 81, my translation from the Italian translation of the Russian)

It should not be presumed that a person will be closer to being spontaneous and to the possibility of contact with the environment when speaking a native language. As with other modes and forms of belonging, calling into question and reformulating one's communication skills by learning a new language can lead to greater self-awareness.

> For instance [...], a child learning to speak has an angry mother, finds that certain words or certain subjects, or even babbling itself, are dangerous; he distorts, conceals, or inhibits his expression; eventually he stammers, and then, because this is too embarrassing, represses the stammering and learns to speak again with other emergency mouth parts. It is generally agreed that such a history of speech-habits importantly constitutes the split-personality of a person; but we here want to call attention not to the fate of the personality but to the fate of the speech. As his experience widens in society, the arts and sciences, our speaker makes higher and wider verbal abstractions. Must it not be the case that, since he is still blotting out the awareness and paralyzing the expression of the lower preverbal connections, he will have defective contact with the actual functioning of

the higher abstractions, both of their meaning to *himself* and also of what they really are? They do have a meaning, yet they do exist, ultimately, in a void. They are "mental."

(Perls et al. 1994, pp. 43–44)

Even speaking, dwelling in one's native language, can be detached from life and thus limit the potentiality for contact, presence, change, and evolution. When stepping into a new language, there is the risk of using concepts devoid of experience, but there is also the possibility of gaining greater spontaneity and flexibility. This latter polarity constitutes a way of starting all over again, connecting individual words, entire sentences, discourses, dialogues, and silences with experience. It is a possibility that comes especially where there is a relational drive, an interest in becoming a part of a new context, one that is also linguistic.

Shared languages

Migration processes disrupt constructed linguistic equilibria more abruptly than other novelties. Learning a language is a very different experience when the new environment actively interacts with the individual, to when the social and linguistic context is completely impermeable and ossified, demanding of foreigners that they simply adapt and survive, without engaging in a process of reciprocal harmonization. Relational intentionality plays a fundamental role in the learning of a language, both for individuals and for groups. Consider the apparently trivial experience of taking lessons in a foreign language and think of how variable our progress is as learners depending on the relationship with the teacher, on how we judge the teacher and are judged in turn, on whether the teacher encourages our efforts or stresses our mistakes. We also know that by sharing experiences, people construct a shared language. Being part of a group—society as a whole, a workplace, a circle of friends—involves a mutual and linguistic creative adjustment. The same process occurs in couples and in families, where adjustment, the effort to adapt to the other, and even nullify oneself in the process, is not always the most conducive means for encounter, exchange, and connection, for an authentic, enriching, and creative experience.

Let's consider one last aspect. Linguistic exchange is a process that does not always necessarily unfold with other people. Watching a movie, perceiving an advertising message, or reading a book can similarly be moments of contact and contamination, which, when re-experienced and gone through, become part of a richer and more meaningful ground. In turn, a movie, a book, or a cultural product are the outcomes of previous contact processes and exchanges.

Acknowledging that aesthetic experience actually modifies who undergoes it entails the problem of mediation between the work and the world of the reader. Moreover, once it is acknowledged that the work is encountered in the world (of the reader), the way is opened for acknowledging, as we saw, that it, in turn, came to be in a world and it bears that world inside itself in some way; the work is true, i.e., it is part of my reality now, because it was true to begin with, it came to be as part of a reality and it bears that reality in itself, in transmuted form. Once the work is removed from the isolation in which aesthetic consciousness situated it, its experience becomes a problem of mediation between two worlds, the world of the work and the world of the reader; that is, it is a hermeneutical problem.

(Vattimo 2001, p. xiv, my translation)

Being open to experience, to the stratification of meanings present, actually or potentially, in a text, in history, in the urban environment, in the life of a place, can create a sense of dizziness. The impact is strong and transformative. The sensation is that of becoming a protagonist in that story, in that building, in those cultural processes. Meanings are constructed that become part of the narrative.

Language thrives on contaminations and as such it is an unfolding of a great many hermeneutical stratifications, of a great many stories of sharing, encounter, and conflict. The intercultural approach facilitates us in moving closer to these processes, at once mysterious and revelatory. Speech throbs with life once again.

Closing the circle, let's end this chapter the way we began it. With poetry.

What is purely bidden in mortal speech is what is spoken in the poem. Poetry proper is never merely a higher mode (*melos*) of everyday language. It is rather the reverse: everyday language is a forgotten and therefore used-up poem, from which there hardly resounds a call any longer.

The opposite of what is purely spoken, the opposite of the poem, is not prose. Pure prose is never "prosaic." It is as poetic and hence as rare as poetry.

(Heidegger 1971, p. 208)

Notes

1 According to Daniel Stern (1985), the early development of the self unfolds in stages connected with progressive interactions between the mother and infant. Stern calls these stages the emergent self (0–4 months), the core self (2–6 months), the subjective self (7–12 months), the verbal self (15–18 months), and the narrative self (3–4 years).

2 "With the development of language, during the second year of life, a new means of exchange is formed that allows shared meanings between the mother and infant to be created. As Stern rightly cautions, however, language 'drives a wedge between two simultaneous forms of interpersonal experience: as it is lived and as it is verbally represented.' Since not all the experiences undergone in the relationship with the mother can be embraced within the verbal field, if not partially, it follows that language will inevitably cause a split in the experience of the self, as it shifts the

experience from the emotional level to the representational level. In this interaction between knowledge (the meanings) and words (signifiers), an essential role is naturally played by the parents and the environment as mediators of culture. To this extent, learning itself can be considered a way of creating shared meanings between adults and infants. This allows us to consider language along the lines of a transitional phenomenon, that is, as the common space necessary for the parent and infant to shape and organize shared meanings. Returning, however, to the split that language creates, as it represents only a part of the multitude of nonverbal experiences, it implies a gap between knowledge of the world (meanings) and words (signifiers)." (Mancia 1988, my translation)

3 "Ethnopsychiatry, between knowledge and experience. Questioning identity, affiliations, and borders" (Turin, 22–23 March 2002), conference organized by Centro Frantz Fanon, ASL I Torino.

4 "By semilingualism we mean the substandard acquisition of two languages, that is, a deficient or imprecise competence in both L1 and L2, for which semilingual speakers do not reach, in either of the two languages, a level of competence equivalent to that of native speakers. [...] Semilingualism is the outcome of a linguistic deconstruction that can be attributed to the power imbalance between the languages of the dominant cultures and the languages of the dominated cultures. Studies by C.B. Paulston in the United States and P. Toukomaa in Scandinavia stress how semilingualism should not be confused with forms of mental weakness or language disorders, but is instead a proper hypothesis for interpreting linguistic deficits in kids who speak minority languages, whether migrants or not, during the schooling process. In the past, such deficits were cited as proof of the perilousness of early bilingual education" (Di Carlo 1994, p. 102, my translation).

References

Baxter P.T.W., Almagor U. (eds.) (1978). *Age, Generation and Time*. New York: St. Martin's Press.
Beneduce R. (1998). *Frontiere dell'identità e della memoria. Etnopsichiatria e migrazioni in un mondo creolo*. Milan: FrancoAngeli.
Benjamin W. (1962). *Angelus Novus. Saggi e frammenti*. Turin: Einaudi.
Benjamin W. (1986). "On Language as Such and On the Language of Man." In *Reflections. Essays, Aphorisms, Autobiographical Writings*. Translated by Edmund Jephcott. New York: Schocken Books, 1986, pp. 314–332
Bernardi B. (1984). *I sistemi delle classi d'età*. Turin: Loescher.
Di Carlo S. (1994). *Proposte per una educazione interculturale*. Naples: Tecnodid.
Gecele M., Francesetti G. (2007) "The Polis as the Ground and Horizon of Therapy." In G. Francesetti (ed.), *Panic Attacks and Postmodernity. Gestalt Therapy Between Clinical and Social Perspectives*. Milan: FrancoAngeli, pp. 170–209. Originally published as "La polis come 'ground' e orizzonte della terapia. In G. Francesetti (ed.) *Attacchi di panico e postmodernità, la psicoterapia della Gestalt fra clinica e società*. Milan: FrancoAngeli, 2005.
Geertz C. (1973). *The Interpretation of Cultures*. New York: Basic Books. Translated in Italian as *Interpretazione di culture*. Bologna: Il Mulino, 1998.
Heidegger M. (1973). *In cammino verso il linguaggio*. Milan: Mursia.
Heidegger (1971). "Language." In *Poetry, Language, Thought*. Translated by Alfred Hofstadter. New York: Harper & Row, pp. 187–210
Hounkpatin L. (2002). "Identità nascoste, identità svelate." In M. Gecele (ed.) *Fra saperi ed esperienze. Interrogare identità, appartenenze e confini*. Turin: Il leone verde.

Lévinas E. (1990). "Loving the Torah more than God." In *Difficult Freedom. Essays on Judaism*. Translated by Seán Hand. Baltimore: The John Hopkins University Press, 1990, pp. 142–146. Originally published as "Aimer la Torah plus que Dieu" in *Difficile liberté. Essais sur le judaïsme*. Paris: Albin Michel, 1995, pp. 189–193. Translated in Italian as *Difficile libertà*. Milan: Jaca Book, 2004.

Lotman Ju. M., Uspenskij B. A. (1977), "Myth—Name—Culture." In D. P. Lucid (ed. and trans.), *Soviet Semiotics: An Anthology*. Baltimore-London: The John Hopkins University Press, 1977, pp. 233–252

Lotman J.M., Uspenskij B.A. (2001). *Tipologia della cultura*. Milan: Bompiani.

Mancia M. (1988). "Recensione di Il mondo interpersonale del bambino di D. Stern." *L'Indice* 6.

Merleau-Ponty M. (2012). *Phenomenology of Perception*. Translated by Donald A. Landes. Oxon, UK: Routledge. Translated in Italian as *Fenomenologia della percezione*. Milan: Bompiani, 2005.

Moro M.R., Revah-Levy A. (1998). "Soi-meme dans l' exil. Les figures de l' altérité dans un dispositif psychotérapique." In O. Douville, A. Eiguer, E. Lecourt, M.R. Moro, A. Revah-Levy (eds.) *Différence culturelle et souffrances de l'identité*. Paris: Dunod.

Nathan T., Stengers I. (1996). *Medici e stregoni*. Turin: Bollati Boringhieri.

Ortega y Gasset J. (1992) "The Misery and the Splendour of Translation." Translated by Elizabeth Gamble Miller. In R. Schulte, J. Biguenet (eds.), *Theories of Translation: An Anthology of Essays from Dryden to Derrida*. Chicago/London: University of Chicago Press, 1992, pp. 93–112.

Perls F.S., Hefferline R.F., Goodman P. (1994). *Gestalt Therapy. Excitement and Growth in the Human Personality*. Gouldsboro ME: The Gestalt Journal Press. Translated in Italian as *Teoria e pratica della terapia della Gestalt*. Rome: Astrolabio, 1971.

Razza C. (2001). "La sconfitta del luogo comune. Ortega e la traduzione." In J. Ortega y Gasset *Miseria e splendore della traduzione*. Genoa: Il melangolo, pp. 7–25.

Sichera A. (2001). "A confronto con Gadamer: per una epistemologia ermeneutica della Gestalt." In M. Spagnuolo Lobb (ed.) *La psicoterapia della Gestalt. Ermeneutica e clinica*. Milan: FrancoAngeli.

Stern D.N. (1985). *The Interpersonal World of the Infant: A View from Psychoanalysis and Developmental Psychology*. London: Routledge.

Vattimo G. (2001). *Introduzione*. In H.G. Gadamer *Verità e metodo*. Milan: Bompiani.

7 Novelty, Familiarity, Support
Relational Intentionality in Creative Adjustment

Do we know what is new?

The analysis of migration processes and a focus on foreigners allow us to explore the risks and opportunities of the relationship with what is novel and diverse. But what is novelty? The answer is far from obvious. Novelty is not necessarily recognized and seen as such. Diversity—the complete opposite of what is familiar to us—can be a locus of utopia, of what is idealized or demonized, and in this sense, it can be part of a known narrative, of processes already incorporated into our life horizons. Vice versa, true novelty can be an experience undergone without realizing it, a diverse point of view that makes us redefine our previous pathways. Besides being novel in themselves, an encounter, a relationship, or a situation can determine such a broader restructuring or give the support to make it possible.

Assimilating novelty is transformative and unpredictable in its import. It is not about adding information, interpreting it according to previous patterns, but about becoming others, in continuity with the self. From a relational perspective, novelty is not so much or just something we bump into outside of us; it is above all what is produced, what is accomplished in the encounter.

Any stimulus, experience, and notion can be transformative (Spagnuolo Lobb 2007a) if it is possible to grasp it and relate it to past encounters, to what we have become—if the self, which encompasses the intentionality and direction unfolding here and now, acts spontaneously,[1] without blocks and constraints, albeit within the coordinates marked out by roles, memory, history, and responsibility. Encountering novelty implies dwelling in the experience authentically and with awareness, without slipping automatically into known patterns.

A support for facing up to novelty

Coming truly into contact with the other, with novelty, always entails a certain amount of risk. In order for the space-time of the encounter to be created, which makes it possible for relational intentionality to unfold, and for the encounter to determine a new personal, relational, social, and political

DOI: 10.4324/9781003568292-7

equilibrium, adequate support is necessary. What gives such support? It is given by the relationship itself, by affective bonds, experiences, roles, affiliations, language, habits, knowledge, by the meaning we attach to our life and to our existence in the world, by relational intentionality.

> Thanks to such support, we can even bear the distress that comes from the experience of a sense of limitation and suffering that are inevitably connected with many life experiences. All the sudden and continuous changes of role and context in everyday life can come with a sense of interruption and loss, which is not always vitalized by the flow of awareness. This is true all the more so for "major" experiences of breakage and change concerning us directly or our family. These burdens, these treasures of past experience, are often gone through emotionlessly, with a dull tone, unless something or somebody, in connecting with the custodian of these worlds, makes a contribution to reactualizing and revitalizing them.
> (Gecele 2008, pp. 181ff., my translation)

Of course, for the encounter with novelty to be such, it is also important not to be hungry, tired, thirsty, in danger, or to be in situations of emergency. For in conditions in which primary needs prevail, presence in the world has different implications, targeted first and foremost at restoring vital functions and exchanges.

If there is insufficient support, even the most trivial stimulus, just like the most potentially transformative experience, will fail to occasion change. Instead, previous ideas and beliefs can be reinforced, or notions and thought patterns may add to or overlap with existing ones, or, alternatively, they may be rejected and expelled. The possibility of going through truly enriching and life-changing experiences, contact, and relationships requires the presence of support able to underpin continuity, bonds, consistency with history, roles, affiliations, and values, while helping to cope with and assimilate novelty, change, and the search for new forms and equilibria. "For a new tie of belonging to form, the preexistent networks of belonging, which provide the necessary support for the contact process, must, at least in part, be deconstructed in order to allow the new figure to emerge (Mione et al. 2007, p. 157).

Between desire and fear

Novelty, when it truly is such, triggers and stimulates change. It is inconvenient, and therefore it can elicit desire but also fear. Let's stop and think about this combination of desire and fear. What is considered and described as an aspiration for change and novelty is often such only within certain parameters, coordinates, and conditions that one wishes or believes it necessary to hold firm. The urge for adventure, for instance, does not consider the loss of the most basic certainties that adventure may entail; an interest in the exotic does not contemplate the possibility of giving up what is essentially taken for granted. As an example, think of how ambiguous it is to wish that another person—usually one's partner—would change. The implicit wish is for the other to match our desires more closely, not for him or her truly to fulfil the possibility of being different from us, and hence be an obstacle, a limit, a wound, or a source of fertile openings that cannot be predicted in advance. Similarly, when we 'fall in love' with very different others—not just a partner, but the exoticism we see in people and cultures from far away, what we usually seek is fulfilment, not change.

> The "new" frightens us but it offers us the only way to broaden our experience and express our potentials. "Where there is true novelty there are feelings of interest and fear."[2] Retreating into the familiar or fleeing into the novel are temptations that continuously emerge to avoid feeling the devastating grips of fear-terror. For this not to happen, it is necessary to accept the dynamic process of growth, which unfolds over three inseparable moments that mark out the genuine maturing of the person: structuring, destructuring, restructuring.
>
> (Salonia 2007, p. 154, my translation)

It is easy to confuse and overlap the concepts of novelty and stimulus. Living in contexts characterized by continuous and overlapping stimulations raises the risk of desensitization, with the consequent need for ever-stronger and continuous stimuli. But this ephemeral and inconsistent drive towards 'novelty' is not the same as the drive that leads to encounter with otherness. Above all, new and known, change and stability, risk not matching up with their own narratives. Such a distortion has major implications, as new and known are the polarities through which life moves. They are at once the starting point and end point in experiences and bonds.

In a narcissistic society, the importance of undergoing first-hand experience personally prevails over continuity, construction, and constant effort. As such, emphasis and support are focused on the approach to novelty, or at least so it would appear. As a result, what lies on the side of intimacy and closeness is often belittled, also because it is tied to the manifestation of needs, frailties, and limits. On the other hand, with the situation today in which narcissism consumes itself and becomes fragmentary, even the other, apparently opposite polarity is reinforced. The fragmentation of society leads to value being placed on safety, stability, and belonging—factors that, if not situated within a relational space, risk transforming into fundamentalism. In turn, desensitization leads to the non-perception of the consequences of rigidity and fundamentalism.

Fixity, rigidity, fragmentation, and disorientation

One of the risks raised by fragmentation is the apparent paradox of determining rigid figures that are increasingly detached from the ground and, in a vicious circle, from any possibility for change. Rigid figures and forms can be found in the dynamics between the sexes, in family structures and work arrangements, in roles, in society, even in political organizations. On the contrary, if support is given to the ground in the therapeutic encounter, just as at the social and political levels, the process leads to the formation of new figures that are connected with and nourished by the context and by what remains in the shadows. The ground is supported by not denying complexity, by going through the nuances of every situation and phenomenon with awareness.

> But in fact the self is only apparently invested by the weak figure, for *the self is not the figure it creates but the creating of the figure*: that is, the self is the dynamic relation of ground and figure. Therefore, the therapeutic method, which can only strengthen the self, is to insist on relating the foreground weak-figure (e.g., a man's concept of himself) to its ground, to bring the ground more fully into awareness. Suppose, for instance, the foreground is a verbal rationalization that is clung to. The therapeutic question must be, not whether the proposition is true or false (thus setting up a conflict of objects), but what is the motive for this use of words.
> (Perls et al. 1994, pp. 191–192)

Prejudices are a part of the way we orient ourselves in the world on the basis of sedimented knowledge. They are, therefore, useful. However, when they are not called into question, when they are not treated as orientational devices but as elements of absolute truth and reality, excessive rigidity can develop. This risk, as we have already seen, is all the greater the more the social context is marked by fragmentation and disorientation. Fixity and rigidity mean that an individual, a group, or a community does not use its potentials and resources as best it can. Migration phenomena have become so widespread that they can, in turn, aggravate disorientation and rigidity when they intersect with a fragmented context.

The familiarity of novelty

In the first part of this chapter, it was observed how contact with the 'novel' always implies a certain amount of risk, but what we are discovering is that this is neither entirely nor always true. A known social setting, a sense of belonging experienced, or a consolidated role can be the bearers of a history of adjustments to the environment, made up of withdrawals and giving up, of forced and difficult adaptations—a history of impediments and limits to presence. In every context we learn up to what point we can express ourselves creatively and with whom, perhaps progressively 'daring' more as we gradually sense the relationships and environment—of which we are ceaselessly an active part—able to support new figures and forms. All this can start over from scratch, for a brief lapse of time at least, in a new cultural setting, in a different environment, when the preformed blocks that clutter up the self and the field make way for an expanding potentiality, a true possibility for rebirth in the here and now of experience.

Expanding this perspective, it can be said that while, on the one hand, we bear in us a multitude of reference contexts, which often tone down and lower the degree of novelty given by a new environment, on the other there also exists a history, a sedimentation of roles and shared experiences which also concern contact with novelty, and so it is possible to have a greater or lesser accustomation with novelty. This is only apparently a contradiction in terms. Among the known roles in the networks of belonging we each have, there is, somewhat paradoxically, that of not belonging, of projecting ourselves towards an elsewhere that is, therefore, familiar as much as it is novel.

> In that tranquil noonday Marianna asks herself if she could ever possess this landscape, make a home for herself, a refuge. Now everything is strange to her and therefore valued. But for how long can she expect things around her to remain foreign, perfectly intelligible, yet far away and impossible to decipher?
>
> This withdrawal from the future which is sealing her fate, will it be too great a challenge for her strength? This wish to wander, to meet different kinds of people, is there something arrogant about it, something a little frivolous and perverse? Where will she go to make a home for herself when every home seems too sunk in its roots, too predictable? She would like to be able to carry her home on her back like a snail and go off into the unknown.
>
> (Maraini 1998, p. 234)

The sense of connection with the environment, the support given by feeling that there can be acceptance for us in the world, for our thoughts and for our emotions, can be found in both familiar contexts and in environments that would appear more foreign and remote but akin. Often, sharing interests, values, and ideologies can give a greater sense of connection than sharing the same national or geographical origin. This can be confusing. It can make us believe we are open to novelty and difference, where instead we are looking for affinity and recognition. Such affiliations can be found today between globalization and fragmentation, alongside nationalisms and particularisms, but they only apparently cut across them.

As I said, coming face-to-face with novelty can prove to be more or less stimulating, more or less familiar. Such variability is also connected with the possibility of tolerating excitement, and hence with the presence of relative support. Difficulty in going through excitement and other emotions is indicative of a lack of adequate support, but it can also be a sign of such a presence and exposure at the contact boundary as to make the novelty to be assimilated too much and too great, even in more familiar contexts. The beauty of a new sunset, a smile, a provocation, or an insult can elicit different degrees of reaction depending on the level of sensitivity and exposure to the environment, to the continuous transformation and creation of reality, the world, people, and relationships.

In turn, as we saw earlier, the need for novelty is sometimes correlated with a difficulty in feeling needs and emotions. We have already spoken of the risk of desensitization found in fragmented societies, of the raising of the bar for perceiving stimuli. Today, true novelty may lie in the warmth of belonging, in being able to stay with the simple things, in welcoming emotions and sentiments that speak in whispers.

Constructed polarities

Novelty, therefore, is not always the counterpoint to what is known, familiar, and shared. Thus, we find ourselves faced with complex definitions and phenomena, where polarities are not so fixed. This is also true for another two terms that apparently stand in a relation of antithetical polarity: modernity and tradition.

In the 'Western' world, there is often a tendency to posit the traditional cultural models of others in contraposition not so much to an own cultural tradition, but to a worldview based on a 'scientific' mindset and on socio-economic models presented and posed as univocal and valid for all at all times. In adopting such a lens, however, we paradoxically take up the same static and rigid positions we believed we had eliminated.

> Others, the other societies that historically came before the most significant turning point for humankind or which still today lag behind in pre-Modern conditions, appear [...] to be societies that are irreparably closed and obscurantist, immersed in magical, or at most religious beliefs, ensnared in their superstitions, fettered by their traditions. If the true and authentic sense of humanity is concentrated in the modern, open society, it is inevitable that others end up seemingly not so far at all from the "brute state." We might well be open and laic, always willing to undermine our acquisitions, to overthrow and destroy our certainties, but in this self-centred laicism there is a huge, unchallengeable, and indisputable certainty: that such laicism is ours and ours alone and it is precisely why we represent the highest and most authentic form of humanity; the others do not know what laicism is and are not capable alone of freeing themselves from the bleak burden of customs and beliefs, which is precisely why they instantiate inferior, lesser, and less authentic forms of humanity. [...]. Dominated as we have been (including many anthropologists) by the paradigm of "Us laics (modern and rational) *vs.* the others (ritualists and traditionalists)," we have never thought to equip ourselves to grasp, even amongst those others, their own forms, degrees, and types of laicism. And to think that it was no less than one of the founding fathers of cultural anthropology, Franz Boas, at the end of the eighteen hundreds, who posited as one of the tasks of the new science to "observe

the fight of individuals against tribal customs," as the kind of struggle that the individual genius "has to undergo among ourselves in his battle against dominant ideas or dominant prejudice" is the same as the struggle elsewhere of a strong individual "to free himself of the fetters of convention." The BaMbuti (the BaMbuti! "Pygmies") are renowned in the anthropological literature for their refractoriness towards ideas of witchcraft and for their remarkable level of anti-ritualism, such as to be compared to the modern people of London. The Tonga people of Zambia show a very laic pragmatism towards their "rain shrines," whose effectiveness is mercilessly checked against the facts—if it does not rain, they are rather quick to abandon the spirit to which the shrine is dedicated and turn to another one.

(Remotti 2006, pp. 48ff., my translation)

Reminders that allow us to consider our own beliefs, symbols, and conceptions as being the outcome of an uninterrupted and vital process within a cultural, religious, and philosophical tradition are therefore important. If we truly feel we are part of a story, of a process that encompasses us but does not end with us, it is easier to seek encounter with people travelling along other pathways, no matter how different they may be. Even within the sphere of interfaith dialogue, often it is the person more deeply engaged in his/her religious experience—with all the certainties, questions, and doubts that entails—who is closer to the encounter with someone who comes from a different relationship with the sacred and divine.

Continuity and transformation in cultures: Contacts and circularity

Let's recall how culture can be considered an organizer of both the continuity and the transformation of a group—of the transmission processes that unfold within it and of the exchanges that bring renewal to the group and connect it with the outside. Human groups self-represent themselves in a self-representation that, determined by multiple contacts and connections, is also the fruit of how the outside, the 'foreigner,' constructs its representation of groups to which it does not belong.

Think, for example, of the African 'traditions' that were constructed in the folds of colonialism and, more generally, of the concept of 'invented traditions,' introduced in 1983 with the publication of *The Invention of Tradition*, a multidisciplinary book edited by Eric Hobsbawm and Terence Ranger (1983). In his introduction, Hobsbawm asserts that "'Traditions' which appear or claim to be old are often quite recent in origin and sometimes invented." Connecting them to the past serves to give them greater legitimacy and authoritativeness.

What is often truly new, and astonishing, is to bring out the myriad facets of interconnected and stratified relations, of the interplay of mirrors, constructions, and reciprocal cross-references that were introduced earlier, in the chapter on 'Othernesses.' Disentangling it all, at every turn our certainties and commonplaces wobble. Staying fully with this process of revelation risks leaving us without foundations.

> Worn out by following the talk that whirled around me, I had begun to feel drowsy when the discussion turned to China. But I did not have to exhaust myself further, for several of the guests knew better than I what was or what should be a Chinese. As a matter of fact, one of them, after listening to me for a moment, proclaimed without preamble: "How odd, you aren't very Chinese!" Other fine minds, claiming expertise, issued pronouncements on Chinese thought, Chinese poetry, Chinese art. Listening to them I finally caught on to what it was they demanded of a Chinese. They wanted a creature with his head in the clouds, untroubled, unquestioning, his face smooth and flat, his smile beatific, a creature of a substance other than flesh and blood. He should be chatty, speaking naturally and without much forethought, avoiding carefully crafted phrases; his comments should be simple and rather naive, leading up to some amiable nugget of wisdom. In short, an unsophisticated being, destined to remain a bumpkin, condemned to a life with neither passion nor the desire to explore new worlds.
>
> Once I had left the dinner party, I breathed in the cool, fresh air and swore they would never again catch me unawares. I told myself sternly that I would have to be more Chinese, that I would have to try to fit their idea of a Chinese.
>
> (Cheng 2000, p. 137)

Art as a locus of multiplicity, as a voice of the field

As I stressed when speaking about language, experiences, relationships, and processes in which the self continuously forms and renews itself include encounters not only between concrete people. Encounters are also made with the authors of the books we read, with the directors and actors of the movies we watch, with the characters of the fairytales we read as children. Reading and engagement with other forms of art brings us face-to-face with the stratification of meanings and experiences found in every art work. We also are and have something of the people and social groups we have never encountered and never will, but which we have imagined and constructed through countless relational and experiential contexts. All these roles, affiliations, and memories sum up to form our view of humans and humanity—the ground present, *a priori*, in every new encounter.

Artistic expressions are part of the language, texts, and codes of a culture, but they are also, at the same time, boundary mechanisms. As such, they constitute a metalanguage, pointing to an elsewhere that is never entirely definable or speakable. Literature can make familiar and approachable even what is distant. It helps us understand distance through proximity, but also proximity through distance. It is not a question of taming the unknown and making it known, but of broadening the space and possibilities of listening, of broadening the horizon of the possible, to the point of creating and inhabiting new worlds. We respond to stories and tales, even those coming from distant, foreign lands and people, through other stories—which open a listening ear for silence, a space for what is hidden, and worlds to inhabit beyond distances.

> Thanks to literature, to the consciousness it shapes, to the desires and longings it inspires, and to our disenchantment with reality when we return from the journey to a beautiful fantasy, civilization is now less cruel than when storytellers began to humanize life with their fables. We would be worse than we are without the good books we have read, more conformist, not as restless, more submissive, and the critical spirit, the engine of progress, would not even exist. Like writing, reading is a protest against the insufficiencies of life. When we look in fiction for what is missing in life, we are saying, with no need to say it or even to know it, that life as it is does not satisfy our thirst for the absolute [...].
>
> Let those who doubt that literature not only submerges us in the dream of beauty and happiness but alerts us to every kind of oppression, ask themselves why all regimes determined to control the behavior of citizens from cradle to grave fear it so much they establish systems of censorship to repress it and keep so wary an eye on independent writers. [...]
>
> Good literature erects bridges between different peoples, and by having us enjoy, suffer, or feel surprise, unites us beneath the languages, beliefs, habits, customs, and prejudices that separate us.
>
> (Vargas Llosa 2011, pp. 7–8)

This is one of the possible conclusions to our journey. There could be many others. Or perhaps there is no conclusion, but just rests, moments of possible assimilation. To then set off again and come face-to-face with familiarity and novelty, just as in life.

Notes

1 "Autonomy must not be confused with spontaneity. It is free choosing, and has always a sense of primary disengagement followed by commitment. The freedom is given by the fact that the ground of the activity has already been achieved: one commits oneself according to what one *is*, that is, has become. But the middle mode of spontaneity does not have the luxury of this freedom, nor the feeling of security that comes from knowing what and where one is and being able to engage or not; one *is* engaged and carried along, not in spite of oneself, but beyond oneself. Autonomy is less extrinsically active than deliberateness and of course less extrinsically passive than relaxation—for it is one's own situation that one engages in according to one's role." (Perls et al. 1994, p. 161)

2 Perls L. (1989). *Leben der Grenzen*. Cologne: Humanistiche Psycologie.

Reference List

Cheng F. (2000). *The River Below*. Translated by Julia Shirek Smith. New York: Welcome Rain.

Gecele M. (2008). "Incontri con l'alterità. Il terapeuta della Gestalt fra il decentramento culturale e la responsabilità sociale." In A. Ferrara, M. Spagnuolo Lobb (eds.) *Le voci della Gestalt. Sviluppi e innovazioni di una psicoterapia*. Milan: FrancoAngeli.

Hobsbawm E., Ranger T. (eds.) (1983) *The Invention of Tradition*, Cambridge University Press, Cambridge. Translated in Italian as *L'invenzione della tradizione*. Turin: Einaudi, 1987.

Maraini D. (1998). *The Silent Duchess*. Translated by Dick Kitto and Elspeth Spottiswood. New York: The Feminist Press at The City University of New York. Originally published as *La lunga vita di Marianna Ucria*. Milan: Rizzoli, 1992.

Mione M., Conte E., Francesetti G., Gecele M. (2007). "Networks and Processes of Belonging: Between Roots and Intentionalities." In G. Francesetti (ed.), *Panic Attacks and Postmodernity. Gestalt Therapy Between Clinical and Social Perspectives*. Milan: FrancoAngeli, pp. 170–209.

Perls F.S., Hefferline R.F., Goodman P. (1994). *Gestalt Therapy. Excitement and Growth in the Human Personality*. Gouldsboro ME: The Gestalt Journal Press. Translated in Italian as *Teoria e pratica della terapia della Gestalt*. Rome: Astrolabio, 1971.

Remotti F. (2006). "Il pregio di ciò che manca e la laicità degli altri." In G. Preterossi (ed.) *Le ragioni dei laici*. Rome/Bari: Laterza.

Salonia G. (2007). *Odòs*. Bologna: EDB.

Spagnuolo Lobb M. (2007a). "La relazione terapeutica nell'approccio gestaltico." In P. Petrini, A. Zucconi (eds.) *La relazione che cura*. Rome: Alpes Italia, 527–536.

Vargas Llosa M. (2011). *In Praise of Literature and Reading. The Nobel Lecture, December 7, 2010*. Translated from the Spanish by Edith Grossman. New York: Farrar, Straus and Giroux.

Hunger and Doubt: Afterword

Francesco Remotti

There are various activities that, for their way of proceeding and for the objectives they set themselves, cannot but entail some view of humankind, as well as of the world. It could perhaps be argued that everything we do is conditioned by anthropological assumptions that are, for the most part, implicit and undeclared. Thus Mary Douglas, for example, in *Purity and Danger*, a groundbreaking work from 1966, opened our eyes to the implicit—and exquisitely anthropological—meanings of our hygiene practices and our dietary taboos, where even the most trivial habits and commonplace choices of everyday life refer back to the ways in which we conceive the world and we conceive ourselves in the world and in the midst of others (Douglas 1970). It is cultures, with their various classification systems, which provide these views. Even scientific knowledge, with its underlying paradigms, conveys world views and views of humankind of a notably 'cultural' flavour. A few years before the release of Mary Douglas's *Purity and Danger*, Thomas Kuhn, in his 1962 book *The Structure of Scientific Revolutions*, had made it clear how science was 'normally' guided by 'paradigms,' or general world views whose principles are normally not called into question, being as they are the fruit of conventions and assumptions shared by scientific communities (Kuhn 1962).

Thus, it is not only exotic societies, the tiny villages studied by anthropologists, but also scientific societies that have their culture. In short, culture winds up embracing the less conscious practices of everyday life as much as it does the most sophisticated and regulated intellectual activities, such as those carried out, for example, in scientific laboratories. Culture, or rather, cultures constitute the 'ground,' and it seems it can be said—in line with the concepts presented in this book by Michela Gecele—that there can be no activity, noble or base as it may be, without ground, without culture, and without that most hidden and implicit dimension of culture which, precisely insofar as it is unquestioned and almost naturalized, supports us in our choices, preventing us from remaining stuck at crossroads. And the cultural 'ground'—as was seen with Mary Douglas—implies options that are always greatly significant for the world, for things, and for humanity.

Why such implications? Anthropologists might answer by pointing out that human beings are highly cultural animals—so cultural as to dismiss much of the genetic 'information' that instead largely shapes the behaviour of other species. Genetic information and cultural information are inversely proportional—the more an animal species has relied, in its evolution, on cultural information, the more it has ended up doing away with genetic information. To a certain extent, which varies from species to species, the former has replaced the latter. We can safely say, without fearing contradiction, that *Homo Sapiens* is the species that has gone down this road the furthest. And obviously it will have had good reason to do so, in evolutionary terms. However, what interests us here is to note—as Clifford Geertz claimed in the 1970s (Geertz 1973)—the extreme degree of dependency on culture, or on its cultural 'grounds,' that unmistakably (and worryingly) marks the human condition.

The relationship between cultural information and genetic information is not one of mere mechanical substitution, for there is a considerable structural difference between the two types of information. In particular, cultural information cannot ignore the motivations that give rise to it and the purposes it serves—namely, a profound and underlying disorientation, which it must remedy. The disorientation referred to here concerns the various spheres of human behaviour, the huge multitude of choices and solutions possible, and hence the great diversity of ways with which to give shape to humanity. The cultural information that steers our everyday behaviour (diet, hygiene, sex, relationships, work, play, and so on) inevitably conveys certain ideas of humanity. The fact that these ideas are largely situated in cultural 'grounds' is a way of rendering them active, while at the same time protecting them from social erosion and critical corrosion; a way of safeguarding them and ensuring their continuity and functionality.

It would not be bad, however, to return to what was said at the start of this piece and to ask whether there are any activities that demand, more than others, the activation of anthropological concepts. For if it is true that morning hygiene practices put into action choices of an anthropo-logical and anthropo-poietic nature, it is just as true there are activities that, in a decisively more intense, problematic, and conscious way, activate anthropological choices in the 'ground.' It seems to me that this book by Michela Gecele, addressing the assumptions and implications of Gestalt therapy, goes exactly in this direction.

In short, there is a difference, in terms of anthropological intensity, between morning ablutions and a therapy session attended an hour later. Both of these activities are anthropologically significant, as they evoke choices concerning forms of humanity. Moreover, they are both 'hands on' in dealing with formative processes of humanity. Nevertheless, it is one thing to do up my face and dress up my figure so that, leaving the intimate sphere of my sleep and my home, others can 'recognize' me as an adult woman or as an adult man bearing a certain status and performing a determinate role; it is another to intervene, with 'relational intentionality,' in a process in which the 'making of humanity' in a determinate person has encountered difficulty, meeting with obstacles and generating distress, wounds, and suffering. Precisely because it deals with a pulsating and suffering humanity, 'therapy work' urgently calls not only for intervention techniques, but also tools, ideas, and perspectives that are expressly anthropological to inspire those techniques.

I presume the urgency to put together such an anthropological conception led the author to shift her attention firmly from the therapeutic relationship as such (the technical aspect) to a more general definition of the Self as a system of 'contacts' and as relationality with the other. Both the philosophy underpinning Gestalt therapy and the analyses and insights developed by Gecele in her book belong within a growing mainstream that posits its fundamental principle in the relationality of the Self. Accordingly, the Self cannot be thought of as a substance, endowed with its own autonomy and consistency, but is instead conceived in terms of a process and activity that takes place in a boundary zone, in contact with alterity. From the start, in illustrating the thought of leading authors in the school of Gestalt therapy, Michela Gecele brings to light the motivation underpinning the Self as contact and as relation. Encounter with the other is conceived as 'nourishment' and is characterized by the activity of 'assimilation,' understood along the lines of 'digestion.' This, in turn, is an unconscious and involuntary process, which entails two aspects: on the one hand, the rendering of the contents of otherness and novelty similar to the self; on the other, the transformation of the self, as a result. Only this way does assimilation give rise to what is declared to be its ultimate objective, which is the 'growth' of the individual. Contact itself is conceived not as a conclusive moment, an end in itself, but rather as a stage that is a means to its "functional 'end,' which is assimilation and growth" (Perls et al. 1951, p. 195). Thus, contact is made with otherness in order to assimilate others and transform ourselves, processes that in turn are considered necessary for the more important goal of 'growth.'

In the reconstruction proposed by Gecele, what is striking is a vision of the Self that, though falling within a humanistic perspective, is organicistic in a way, and even alimentational (starting from the organism/environment binary, which recurs extensively in the foundational writings)—a vision or metaphor posited as the basis of the value around which the entire Gestalt therapy agenda revolves, which is 'growth.' In a paper by Spagnuolo Lobb et al. (2001, p. 187), we read: "Every experience of contact is functional for the growth of both the individual and the community." It is a growth that, in the constant search for 'novelty' (the principle of the *now-for-next*) and for the continuous transcendence it entails, finds an essential factor of existential organization. As it clearly appears in Frederick Perls 1947 work, *Ego, Hunger and Aggression* (Perls 1947), 'hunger' takes on paradigmatic value not just at the organic level, but also at the mental level, as the hunger instinct and the satisfaction of the need to eat are the elements that most connect the individual to its environment. Frederick Perls highlighted the existence of 'mental food' and the fact that, even on the psychological plane, there is a "concentration on eating."

From an anthropological perspective, it is hard to ignore a suggestion that might appear out of place and, perhaps, repulsive. Feeding off the other and otherness taken as a locus of choice for mental nutrition induces one to see in this type of thought something not all that far off from anthropophagy. What Gestalt therapy ultimately proposes is a 'feeding on humanity.' It should be specified, perhaps, as Marshall Sahlins did many years ago, that "cannibalism is always 'symbolic,' even when it is 'real'" (Sahlins 1983, p. 88). And once serious consideration is given to the need for food, perhaps it is not so surprising that anthropology itself was ultimately conceived as a form of anthropophagy (Remotti 1988). In truth, it is easy to demonstrate how in practically all cultures, the matter of 'feeding on humanity'—especially 'other' humanity—is a constant that attracts and disturbs us at the same time, and how efforts are made to channel this 'hunger for humanity' into forms that do not develop into a devastating 'aggressiveness.' Even when cannibalism is real, it is highly unlikely to be motivated by a shortage of animal protein, given that what is of absolute importance in cannibalism—as Michel de Montaigne asserted long ago in relation to the Tupinamba in Brazil—is the mental and symbolic component. The highly ritual way in which enemies to be eaten were procured by the Tupinamba, along with the comportment of the captured warrior—who, instead of fleeing, accepted his destiny, so as to bring his humanity to accomplishment in the intimate contact with his enemy, that is, in the very moment in which he would be eaten by 'others'—shows us how profound the anthropological thinking of the Tupinamba was with regard to the relationship between 'us,' our form of humanity, and 'others' bearing another form of humanity (Remotti 1996, Chapters VIII, X).

If we think about it, an anthropological view of an alimentational kind, as sublimated as it may be, opens up a dimension of no small drama. It is no coincidence that Michela Gecele ends up focusing her attention on the problematic of intercultural contacts and the encounter with the foreigner. Here, obviously, the matter of otherness is all the more accentuated and the risks and promises greater. On the basis of the premises discussed earlier, it could be said that the greater otherness is, the greater the promise of growth is. Thus, the phenomenon of immigration winds up assuming paradigmatic value, especially when considered not only in terms of its more contingent motivations but in the dimension it opens up of the journey and venture towards otherness. Immigration, Gestalt therapy, and the practice of anthropological research are connected by nexuses that refer back to each other. Thus, we catch a very clear glimpse in the pages of this book of a parallel, one only barely hidden, between the anthropological enterprise (a journey through otherness) and Gestalt therapy: for both there is an "inclination towards the external, towards otherness"; both represent useful perspectives "for understanding multicultural contexts and for constructing an intercultural agenda."

Regardless of how it is occasioned, "contact with the other," says Michela Gecele, "always entails a certain amount of risk." As such, it would be interesting to draw out from this book expedients that contrast this desire or 'hunger' for otherness, which appears to lie at the foundation of the paradigm examined. They are correctives and rules, via which a more balanced and reassuring outlook is achieved, while above all avoiding the risk of aggressiveness and the risk of being overwhelmed.

The first corrective introduces a criterion of reciprocity and symmetry, so as to prevent nourishment and growth from becoming objectives pursued unilaterally and, in a dyadic relationship, to prevent one partner from prevailing over the other. For predominance would give rise—according to Spagnuolo Lobb, Salonia, and Sichera—to "a neurotic, non-nourishing contact" (2001, p. 187). Nourishment and growth, therefore, are only possible within a relationship of exchange, founded on reciprocity and on symmetry. Gecele asserts that pathology comes from imbalance, from asymmetry. We could add that such a risk is always present, to the extent that the alimentational conception revolves on the pattern of hunger for otherness/contact/assimilation/growth. The risk of seeing and pursuing growth on one's own, exclusively and egocentrically, would appear to be a slippery slope that comes almost naturally, if Gestalt therapy did not step in at that point to warn that it is what lies at the heart of pathologies. To avoid running such a risk, or to remedy this pathogenic stance, Gestalt therapy turns to a principle that, notably, is illustrated in great depth and quite convincingly in classical anthropological thought (commencing especially as of Lévi-Strauss), whereby all social life is conceived in terms of exchange, and exchange—for Lévi-Strauss—finds its golden rule in reciprocity (Lévi-Strauss 1969). We could also integrate the principle of reciprocity with that of 'acknowledgment.' In this case, reciprocity implies acknowledging that even the other is in need of nourishment and growth, which motivates in everybody the search for contact. The anthropophagy of the Tupinamba we mentioned earlier can be taken as a case illustrating this essential point in a particularly effective way: Reciprocity dominates and inspires anthropophagy itself (Remotti 1996).

The second corrective instead introduces an element of discontinuity. As much as the authors cited above insist greatly on growth, they intend growth not as a continuous process, but, on the contrary, as a process interrupted by 'rests.' It cannot be excluded that the organicistic view itself suggests the need for discontinuity. In any case, contact is regularly interrupted, as the phase of 'contact' gives way to 'withdrawal from contact.' Therefore, as important as it is to be inclined towards otherness, to come out towards the other and to open up to the boundary, and thus give rise to assimilation processes, the moment of withdrawal, of relative closure, of silence and refuge, and resting in intimacy, is equally indispensable. To continue with the underlying alimentational view, it could be said that we do not feed on otherness continuously;

the very processes of assimilation and digestion demand we rest from feeding, so that it can be transformed into growth.

On a closer look, the two correctives—that of reciprocity and acknowledgment and that of rest—subject 'hunger' to rules, preventing it from transforming into voraciousness, into a continuous feeding, which would mean not taking into account the hunger of the other, nor the physiological rhythms of feeding. Thus, limits are placed on continuous, unilateral voraciousness and on its disastrous consequences—limits that emerge first in relationships with others, in synchrony, so to speak, and secondly in diachrony, in the temporal unfolding of the activity itself of feeding and growth. While for the first corrective (reciprocity) it was quite simple to find significant confirmation in classical anthropological thought, for the second corrective (rest), examples can be drawn from a slightly less institutional level, but with references that are just as significant.

It was, for instance, Marcel Mauss (who actually inspired the principle of reciprocity), in an essay from way back in 1904–1905, who noticed an alternating rhythm in Eskimo societies in relation to the passage from summer to winter and back again. On the economic plane, the busy hunting and fishing activity of the summer season gave way to winter rest, while on the social plane, the intensive ritual activity of the winter season petered out, to all but disappear during the summer season. For Marcel Mauss, however, this "curious alternation," this "regular rhythm"—as though having a "high point" and a "low point"—that can be observed in Eskimo social life is not confined solely to that society (Mauss 1979, p. 77). On the basis of the Eskimo case and analogous cases he mentions at the end of his essay, Mauss derived a "law" of vast generality, which states that social life cannot be sustained at the same level at all times of the year, thus "it goes through regular, successive phases of increased and decreased intensity, of activity and repose, of exertion and recuperation" (Mauss 1979, pp. 78–79).

There are interesting references in Mauss's essay to the need "to live a more individual life," a calmer, more isolated, and more profane existence, after the communal living, revelries, and social intensity of the long winter months in Eskimo society, when individuals live in such close contact with each other (Mauss 1979, p. 79). If social life is a sort of performance that people act out on the public stage, we can clearly appreciate how the authors who have taken up the theatrical metaphor highlight the need for 'rest,' to exit the stage and retreat—as Erving Goffman (1959) would say—into a "backstage." However, even social life that revolves around exchange and reciprocity is stressful, and it is significant to note how Lévi-Strauss himself highlights the need for "rests" that interrupt the "anxious venture" of exchange, through to evoking the Andaman myth of a situation in which human beings can finally live *"entre soi"*, intimately keeping to themselves (Lévi-Strauss 1969, p. 489, 497). As for myself, it seemed to me that this 'search for intimacy'—this withdrawal from 'contact,' from 'exchange,' from the 'performance' on stage—is a dimension that cannot be renounced, a necessity felt not just on the individual level, but a need to which societies respond in different ways (Remotti 2012). So why not explicitly introduce the theme of 'suspension,' of slowdown, rest, and interruption, as a dimension inherent to cultural organization itself? (Remotti 2011, cap. VIII).

Taking this path, however, we can go even further, to the point of hypothesizing a much broader and more radical rest, one that concerns and calls into question the idea of growth itself. The myth of growth is replaced by Maurizio Pallante (2005) with "happy degrowth," while Serge Latouche (2009) says "farewell to growth." For it is one thing to think of rests as slowing down growth with a view to picking it up again with greater energy; it is another to think of rests as stabilizing a situation in psychological terms and in social (and economic) terms. In response to "growth for the sake of growth" and the "compulsive addiction to growth," these authors put forward the principle of the impossibility of "infinite growth" in a "finite" world, in which resources are limited (Latouche 2009, p. 3). It is true that the advocates of degrowth refer to the myth of growth in financial and economic terms. But shouldn't the idea of a finite world, or the principle of limited possibilities, also concern the psychological sphere and the way the lives of human beings are organized, along with their societies and their cultures?

To conclude, is there truly an irrepressible desire for growth in human beings, or should the contact/feeding/assimilation/growth sequence (the underlying formula of Gestalt therapy) be understood, in its turn, as a culturally conditioned model of humanity—a model, in other words, that is 'creatively adjusted' to the type of society in which it was formulated? If that were the case, it might not be a bad idea to elevate 'doubt'—rather than 'hunger'—to being the key to anthropo-poietic processes. That is the lesson of many initiation rites, where no specific idea of humanity is imposed on young initiates, but rather, for formative purposes, they raise an anthropological doubt, critical spirit, and an awareness that in matters of anthropo-poiesis there are no sure solutions and highways, but nothing more than side streets, narrow lanes, and dead-ends, in which us and them just try to make do. Beyond the question, 'What is a human?', often naught else remains but to express a wish: "That our journey should generate men" (Remotti 2013, p. 199). So the BaNande of northern Kivu (Democratic Republic of Congo) would begin, in the past, the *olusumba*, the anthropo-poietic ritual through which they sought to initiate their youths into manhood and give meaning to their existence.

References

Douglas M. (1970). *Purity and Danger*. Harmondsworth: Penguin Books. Translated in Italian as *Purezza e pericolo*. Bologna: Il Mulino, 1975.

Geertz C. (1973). *The Interpretation of Cultures*. New York: Basic Books. Translated in Italian as *Interpretazione di culture*. Bologna: Il Mulino, 1987.

Goffman E. (1959). *The Presentation of Self in Everyday Life*. Garden City, NY: Doubleday. Translated in Italian as *La vita quotidiana come rappresentazione*. Bologna: Il Mulino, 1969.

Kuhn T. (1962). *The Structure of the Scientific Revolutions*. Chicago: Chicago University Press. Translated in Italian as *La struttura delle rivoluzioni scientifiche*. Turin: Einaudi, 1969.

Latouche S. (2009) *Farewell to Growth*. Translated by David Macey. Cambridge: Polity Press. Originally published as *Petit traité de la décroissance sereine*. Paris: Fayard, 2007. Translated in Italian as *Breve trattato sulla decrescita serena*. Turin: Bollati Boringhieri, 2008.

Lévi-Strauss C. (1969) *The Elementary Structures of Kinship*. Translated by James Harle Bell, John Richard von Sturmer, and Rodney Neddham (ed.). Boston: Beacon Press. Originally published as *Les Structures élémentaires de la parenté*. Paris: Mouton, 1949–1967. Translated in Italian as *Le strutture elementari della parentela*. Milan: Feltrinelli, 1984.

Mauss M. (1979) *Seasonal Variations of the Eskimo: A Study in Social Morphology*. Trans. James J. Fox. London/New York: Routledge. Originally published as "Essai sur les variations saisonnières des sociétés eskimos. Étude de morphologie sociale." *L'Année sociologique* IX (1904–1905), 39–132. Translated in Italian as "Saggio sulle variazioni stagionali delle società eschimesi. Studio di morfologia sociale." In É. Durkheim, M. Mauss *Sociologia e antropologia*. Rome: Newton Compton, 1976, pp. 141–234.

Pallante M. (2005). *La decrescita felice. La qualità della vita non dipende dal PIL*. Rome: Editori Riuniti.

Perls F.S. (1947). *Ego, Hunger and Aggression: A Revision of Freud's Theory and Method*. Highland NY: The Gestalt Journal Press, 1992. Translated in Italian as *L'Io, la fame, l'aggressività*. Milan: FrancoAngeli, 1995.

Perls F.S., Hefferline R., Goodman P. (1951). *Gestalt Therapy: Excitement and Growth in the Human Personality*. Gouldsboro ME: The Gestalt Journal Press, 1994. Translated in Italian as *Teoria e pratica della teoria della Gestalt. Vitalità e accrescimento nella personalità umana*. Rome: Astrolabio, 1971

Remotti F. (1988). "Il cibo degli antropologi." *L'Uomo* I, 1–2, 3–24.

Remotti F. (1996). *Contro l'identità*. Rome/Bari: Laterza.

Remotti F. (2011). *Cultura. Dalla complessità all'impoverimento*. Rome/Bari: Laterza.

Remotti F. (2012). La ricerca dell'intimità. *Fogli Campostrini* III, 3, 17–35.

Remotti F. (2013). *Fare umanità. I drammi dell'antropopoiesi*. Rome/Bari: Laterza.

Sahlins M. (1983). "Raw Women, Cooked Men, and Other 'Great Things' of the Fiji Islands." In P. Brown, D. Tuzin (eds.) *The Ethnography of Cannibalism*. Washington: Society for Psychological Anthropology, pp. 72–93.

Spagnuolo Lobb M., Salonia G., Sichera A. (2001). "Dal "disagio della civiltà" all'adattamento creativo." In M. Spagnuolo Lobb (ed.) *La psicoterapia della Gestalt. Ermeneutica e clinica*. Milan: FrancoAngeli, 180–190.

Index

Note: Page numbers followed by "n" refer to end notes.

Arendt, H. 27

babalawo 57–58
BaMbuti 71
Bauman, Z. 32, 41n6
Benjamin, W. 16, 44, 57
Boas, F. 70
Bruni, L. 20

collective memory 37–38
communication 46–48, 52–53; intercultural 22; value of 45
complexity 30–32; and boundaries 48–49
continuity 34–38, 71–72
cultural anthropology 58
cultural information 76
culture: art and experience 11; concept of 1–2; and humanistic therapies 2–4

decentralization 10–11
Derrida, J. 40
desire and fear 66–67
disorientation 1, 29, 31–33, 37, 46, 68, 76
diversity 13, 15, 40, 65, 76
Douglas, M., *Purity and Danger* 75
drug effect 31
dualism, polarity of 21
duality and triality 14–15, 20–21
Duras, M. 14

Eliot, T. S. 19
emigration 33–35
emptiness 31–32
Eskimo society 80
eye of 'the other' 7–10

face-to-face with otherness 15, 21–23, 26, 29, 45–46, 69, 72–73
figure/contact 29–30
fixity 35–37, 45, 54–55, 68
foreigners 21–23, 52, 65, 71, 78
fragmentation xiii, 1, 29, 32, 36, 46, 67–69
fullness 31, 47
fundamentalism 19–20, 26–27, 31, 37, 45, 67

Gecele, M. 75–79
Geertz, C. 76
genetic information 76
Gestalt therapy xiii, xiv, 2, 10, 29, 41n7, 48, 51, 76–79, 81
globalization xiii, 1, 33, 69
Goffman, E. 80
Goodman, P. 36
ground concept: boundary and prophetic figures 38–39; complexity 30–32; emigration 33–35; emptiness 31–32; figure/contact 29–30; habits 35–37; 'in-between' 27–28; liquidity 32–33; memory and history 37–38; otherness as 28–29; simplification 30–31; and social fictions 39–40; spirituality 40–41; travel process 26–27

Habermas, J. 52–53
habits 35–37
hermeneutics and translation processes 44–46
Hobsbawm, E. and Ranger, T., *The Invention of Tradition* 71
Hounkpatin, L. 57

humanity xiv, 1, 13–15, 17, 39, 44, 55, 70, 72–73, 76–78, 81

identity, concept of 2
'in-between' space 27–28
individual memory 37–38
infant development (Stern) 53–54
infinity 16, 28, 56
intercultural communication 22
Italianness, degrees of 8–10

Jones, E. E. 22

Kuhn, T., *The Structure of Scientific Revolutions* 75

language(s) 44–45, 51–55, 62–63n2, 63n4; bilingualism and life cycle 59–61; as constriction 58–59; ground and direction 53; names and 56–58; and psychotherapy 52–53; pure 44; shared 61–62
Latouche, S. 81
Lévinas, E. 56
Lévi-Strauss, C. 80
linguistic creative adjustment 54–55
liquidity 32–33
literature 15, 71–73
Lobb, S. 77, 79
Loti, P. 18–19
Lotman, J. M. 45

man-woman relationship 13–14
mass migration xiii
Mauss, M. 80
memory and history 37–38
Merleau-Ponty M. 35
migration process 34–35, 59, 61, 65, 68
Miner, H. 6
multiple interconnections xiii
multiple names 58
multiplicity 13, 15, 55, 57, 72–73
mythological description 56–57

Nacirema 6–7
narrative self 53–54
Nisbett, R. E. 22
nonmythological description 56
novelty 17, 36, 65–66; assimilating 65; desire and fear 66–67; familiarity of 68–70; support for 65–66

Nussbaum, M. 1, 4n1–4n2

Oedipal theory xiii
Ottoman empire 18–19

Pallante, M. 81
Pamuk, O. 18
panic attacks 41n3
Perls, F., *Ego, Hunger and Aggression* 77–78
personality disorders 30
polarity 21, 61, 70–71
polis 27–28, 52; boundary figures and prophetic figures 38–39; to spirituality 40–41
power and translatability 47–48
prejudices 7, 11, 37, 68
proper names 56–58
psychopathology 31, 37, 41n7
psychotherapy: language and 52–53; translation in 46–47

reality and truth 19–20
relational immaturity 32
relational intentionality 30, 40, 61, 65–66, 76–77
relationships and contact 28–29
rigidity 33, 55, 67–68

Sahlins, M. 78
Salonia, G. 79
sedimentation 35, 69
self-sufficiency 14, 40
semilingualism 59, 63n4
shared languages 61–62
Sichera, A. 79
simplification 30–31
social disintegration 29, 46
social fictions 39–40
social maturity 39
speech: in human experience and transcendence 55–56; and mythological dimension 56; and names 57–58; power of 54; self-referential 51
spirituality 40–41
Stern, D. 53–54, 62n1–62n2
substance abuse 32

third training approach 10–11
time and space 33–35

translation process: hermeneutics and 44–46; power and 47–48; in psychotherapy 46–47
travel process 26–27
Trinitarian perfection 21

unknowability of otherness 15–17

verbal self 53–54

'West,' rise of 18–19

Yin, Yang, and the Median Void (Cheng) 21

For Product Safety Concerns and Information please contact our EU representative GPSR@taylorandfrancis.com Taylor & Francis Verlag GmbH, Kaufingerstraße 24, 80331 München, Germany

Batch number: 08220873

Printed by Printforce, the Netherlands